SONS
OF MAN

Sons of Man

Akklesiastical writings
BOOK I

Ivsan Otets

Translated from French by Dianitsa Otets

{ akklesia.eu · akklesia.fr · akklesia.com }

© 2023, Ivsan Otets

Edition : BoD - Books on Demand, info@bod.fr
Impression - Printing : BoD - Books on Demand, In de Tarpen 42, Norderstedt (Germany)

Impression à la demande - Printing on demand
ISBN : 978-2-3224-8200-9
Dépôt légal : Août 2023 - First published: August 2023

CONTENTS

FOREWORD AND A BRIEF INTRODUCTION ix

PROLOGUE

    The bridge makers 19

I - SONS OF MAN

    The Four Hearts 23

    What seek ye? 31

    The popes 37

    The Untamable Samson 41

    Vashti the queen 59

    The umbilical cord 65

II - SONS OF LAW (*"them that are perfect"*)

    On the Anglo-American religion 77

    On Billy Graham 85

    On hymns 95

    A geometry of Eden 99

EPILOGUE

    From disciple to ambassador 109

Foreword and a brief introduction

God begets children who are meant to assume His nature **after death**, in their resurrection. Those here below who take on this divine intention for themselves are therefore all at once sons of Man and sons of God.

Christ is the possibility of this birth, of this filiation; he is the possibility to become son of God. He is the door that opens or shuts on divine life after-death. For that reason, as he went through a man's life during the days of his incarnation on earth, he could nonetheless act according to his divine nature.

Divine fulfilment is to become **a free and sovereign being**, in its own reality. This is what Resurrection as announced by Christ is. That reality in resurrection is a **mystery** in the sense that, we believe, it allows the **meeting** of different sovereign realities, namely, **brotherhood**. There is a blatant contradiction to our minds in these combined possibilities.

It is impossible to grasp this resurrected life in the same way it is impossible to grasp the relationship between two gods, between two kingdoms each of which has a king who reigns as a free and sovereign being in his own kingdom: the kingdom *of a god*. What the Bible calls « the Kingdom of God », therefore, is actually *kingdoms of god*s.

Here is in a nutshell the Gospel — the incredible message brought to us by that elusive character we read about in the four Gospels of the New Testament.

As we listen to what Christ **and Christ only** says, this divine *goal* or *main point* or *destination of man* will sound most desirable and eventually « logical », obvious, « natural and coherent » although crazy — because it really is Good News! Absolute Freedom and Sovereignty *and* the possibility of Brotherhood. Let us repeat that there are as many Kingdoms of God as there are sons of God; and to each son of God there is a divine kingdom.

However it is not the way the Gospels have been read and taught throughout the centuries.

Consequently we need to reassess the whole web of explanations, meanings, interpretations, lessons, readings, etc. that we were fed – most of the time in absolute good faith – concerning the Gospels.

That reassessment of the Gospels demands and provokes in turn a great number of readjustments in the ways we were taught to understand many notions, facts and realities: the Bible, faith, history, life, etc.

The story itself of the son of God **as it was written** needs to be reinvestigated in the light of such a resurrection.

✿

We are not the first to declare individual resurrection as being the main and in fact the only message of Christ. In this brief introduction to Akklesia we wish to mention two eminent predecessors to our research: SOREN KIRKEGAARD and LEV SHESTOV.

SHESTOV, for his inspired fight against the invisible albeit unavoidable structures of life here below, which he called « evidences » or « self-evident truths » or realities: Reason and Necessity. They bluntly antagonise man's divine inheritance, Freedom and Sovereignty.

KIRKEGAARD, for his acute writings on the relationship between man and God and for the subsequent penetrating reflection he developped against the established church of his time and place and against the Church in general; not as some potentially toxic political entity, though, but as an institution which is intrinsically opposed to Christ. For KIERKEGAARD the ecclesiastical institution is intrinsically opposed to Christ **because it is a phenomenon of the general**, and because the general is opposed to the individual. Christ *is* the individual. « Christ does not see the crowd », as the Danish philosopher said.

This is where Akklesia starts: in declaring that the Church is **NOT** the « Body of Christ ». It is an assembly with general functions, mostly social and political. It serves as a nursery for newborn believers. The Church indeed functions as a pre-Christ stage, as it were, a function which may be assumed by other institutions.

Ideally, the Church is here to prepare a spiritual child to reach maturity, meaning, to have a relationship with Christ where the tutor – be it the Church, school, society... any general structure – will be left behind. If the Church fails in this mission, it is then holding back an individual, keeping him or her in childhood and barring them from reaching maturity. The Church will subsequently elaborate for them a ghostly, ecclesiastical Christ.

xi

In the case of a failure on the part of the Church in that mission, it is preferable for one to receive morality and consciousness through a neutral structure and to enter in relationship with Christ when He Himself decides it.

Moreover, notwithstanding what some people wrote and included in the Bible, the Church is not some fantasmagorical accretion of persons forming the super-body of another one (be it « superior »)! This is outrageously anti-Christ and anti-man because it goes directly against the divine goal! It is annihilating a person by dissolving him or her into some concept instead of ushering them each in their own free and sovereign Christlike life. For more on the topic of the Church see *The umbilical cord*, pages 65 to 74.

🌿

Central to apprehend the positions adopted by Akklesia is the question of our attitude towards Scriptures.

What the Bible contains is not in our eyes sacred and unerring. The Bible contains inspired and non-inspired material, or: words directly inspired by Christ and words inspired by the spirit of the Tree of Knowledge of good and evil, i.e. Logos and its whole array of politics and propaganda – which has its own function in a man's life. For more on the topic of Scriptures and propaganda see *The Untamable Samson*, pages 41 to 58.

It follows that our attitude vis-à-vis Scripture is to **hunt for the existential murmur of Christ** and to separate it from the roar of the general Logos which is very much present throughout the Bible. Actually, we think that Christ's words only seep through a relatively small part of Scripture.

Some might protest that such an attitude is a slippery slope leading to build fake theology on the basis of personal whims. Our response to that is:

▶ *Firstly* – To quote the phrase often used by US priest and theologian JOHN PAUL MEIER: « *non liquet* » – « *it is not clear* » or « *indeterminate* » (see JP MEIER, *A Marginal Jew: Rethinking the Historical Jesus*, vol. v). By which it must be reminded that biblical writings need interpretation since we are not dealing with the results of a scientific research concluding on irrefutable equations.

And who will dare claim to have supreme authority on one and all so as to authorise or forbid anybody to search, question, probe and study year after year the biblical texts? As for us, we asked permission to no one but to our own hearts to take the charge but also the joy to question the text and to seek God.

In the same volume, MEIER remarks that « many of the parables attributed to Jesus should be assigned to the frustrating no-man's-land of *non liquet*. » (p. 5). Therefore, isn't this « no-man's-land of *non liquet* » actually what God wants? and isn't it that before which the biblical text places us as we study it honestly? And in fact, the more a situation ends up in this ambiguity, the more it prompts us to find another way out in order to solve the equation: a way out into Faith, into God's incarnation and man's divinisation, which no logos can apprehend clearly (« *liquetly* ») nor, in consequence, reproduce. But also, unfortunately, this **non-liquet-truth** situation generates abominations like transhumanism, man's reification, Revelation's cubic city, etc.

And this is why the more separation – which is an action of God, not to say of the *free-spirit* – can take place, the better off we are. — Knowing that **separation** is peculiar to «that which is free», knowing that «this here-free-Spirit» is in truth anti-universalist, anti-globalist, anti-The-One and knowing that he is not obsessed with the hunger to absorb everything into «It, the Unique», since he only wants one thing: that the other be free and sovereign like he is. God, the *free-spirit*, will always prefer five friends of that nature, who would have drunk his blood, than five billion having drunk the ink of logic also drank by the herd sheep, a.k.a the stone which apocalyptic cubes and corpus ekklesias-of-The-One are made of!

But the more that separation occurs, the more ambiguity may also emerge. The logos has always enough technical resources at its disposal and it has *an infinity* of intellectual lies – numbers being **Infinity** by definition – to **simulate** mystery and divinisation. Until, of course, the lie of the logos declaring «I can do as God does» succeeds in having the *homo sapiens* species self-destruct. Which is unavoidable. For numbers are infinite, but only on paper, while flesh and blood disappear from the first lines. This means science may endlessly devise abstract plans – lines after lines of technical code – to imitate God and his project to make man a god after death or at least deeply transform his nature, but as soon as science tries to apply those plans to man, it is destroying him. It seems God has put a limit to man here below so that he can never mutate into what is not Man (a man-machine or a man-electrowave for instance) and still live. Or more precisely, it seems God appointed man's fragile and fleshly nature to be that limit. Therefore the ambiguity is to believe men will succeed in making Man a god by their own strength, with the help of the logos (science, techniques...). Men will only achieve self-destruction in trying. But the « elect » – all those who are **seen** by God – shall exit in time.

▶ *Secondly* – We believe that the biblical text resembles each person: it has a double discourse. The Bible's content really talks about 2 gods, 2 theologies: — A God creator, political, organiser, God of the Logos, etc. — And a God of the individual, of the existing-being, of the mystery of man as a free and sovereign being, etc.

These two spirits mix and get inextricably linked, they combine or fight each other, they work together and perfect each other or disagree totally and absolutely split up — all through Scriptures.

Christ himself used this difficulty when he clearly showed that there were three different ways to encounter God. The way of the Law — which is yet without Christ. The way of Faith — which is the first attempt made by the individual to approach a God that is not Creator. Lastly, the way of the Kingdom of God — which is the way of the divine individual who receives Christ's nature and blood, and who then only knows the God that begets; this person has left far behind himself the organising God of Creation and Laws.

To use a metaphor, Akklesia does not drink Scripture's ink but instead we crush the words of the Bible with the hammer of the existential Christ to see what they give out: living water to carry us forward towards resurrection, or thick and slimy syrup that glues us to general truths and traps us into a false, infantile comprehension of Christ.

This sort of reading is an ongoing, never-ending process, a very delicate activity which **does not go without prayer**. It never is an easy pretext to stack up juicy blogposts or to come up with religious gimmicks.

The Bible is definitely a stumbling block on such a journey as a great number of its words paralyse millions of people into painful perplexity, to the least, or into systematic acquiescence. It is decidedly a source of deep confusion because, as explained earlier, it contains both worldly theology and the living water of Christ.

History of the Scriptures and of Christianity, plus notions such as « fear of God » make it extremely difficult for any believer to consider the words of the Bible in a critical and spiritual manner and to put them in another perspective than those of a textbook: obedience, consolation, coaching, etc. And in the end it is for this very reason that the Bible is a unique and particular book: it offers the contradiction to be either a stumbling block or an entrance, an opening towards that other reality of the God of the individual; it is instrumental in creating this separation. Those who get bogged down in « fear of God » are thus choosing one of these two paths the text proposes. Those who leave the crushing process of the Torah are choosing the other path.

It is true that this possibility to be either a man of the general or an existing-being is a recurring alternative which can be found in philosophy, in literature, in life too!, etc. But the specificity of the Bible is that it depicts the Existing-Being as a being who became flesh (Christ).

The Bible is certainly an inspired text on the whole because it reveals each and every one for what he or she is. And so much the better!

∼

Preparation to resurrection needs a « follower of Christ » to seek actively to lift the curse off him/herself and break the lifelong spell of the Logos. That spell lies in the Torahic and religious outlook which has relentlessly been imposed on all by authorised interpreters of Scriptures, and also by the instinctive reflex man demonstrates to become a son of the Logos instead of a son of God; and of course by society which agrees so well with the Torah-God. Indeed, even when society spreads a humanistic and atheistic message, it is drawing from that Torahic spirit and will accordingly spawn sons of the General.

The twelve texts proposed here are as many instances of such a struggle for « de-spelling » ourselves.

Ivsan & Dianitsa Otets

PROLOGUE

The bridge makers
To world citizens

WHENEVER TWO MEN MEET, Nature creates between them an invisible and sacred river. A river which becomes as narrow as a thin rivulet should these individuals be part of a family sharing the same culture and intellectual values; but which turns into a wide and uncrossable torrent as their race, culture and spiritual values diverge. The same goes for all animals modelled by Nature, although, in their case, the gap that separates them is almost never bridged. Nature, who so much loves thinking and classifying, cannot endure « anarchy » and only in rare instances does she allow a few snags in her classification. Therefore a lion cannot live among gazelles, and in the same way, wolves do not feed from sheep's pastures. For any animal, to cross over the rivers of sacred order will almost always mean death: a transgression they shall pay with their blood. Domesticated beasts can sometimes learn to coexist with their opposite banks, but only with the help of humans, as only man has succeeded, little by little, in building communication bridges between differences. We are **BRIDGE MAKERS**, *pontiffs*, and even Nature's sovereign pontiffs. We are careful to preserve her order all the while building crossovers to connect differences. We create collectivity, that is to say, religion.

Such is our tear: on the one side, Nature's order fascinates us but on the other, her intolerance is intolerable to us. However, by insisting on generating a contractual language between her wild shores to stop the violence of their opposition, we end up erasing any distance between men; we end up creating concentrated camps where every one becomes every one's mirror. We are then continually facing a dilemma: either we dry up all rivers on earth with an excess of communication, thus strangling our own freedoms; or we flood her with powerful water streams so as to mark our distinctiveness and, fatally, we generate conflict! In the end, modern man has no other recourse than the medium way: **LUKEWARMNESS**. He must freeze in the « not too much, not too little » position, right in the middle of a complex calculation. On the one hand, the space between human shores shall not go over the norm authorised by wisemen, and on the other, the intensity of our distinctiveness – that is to say the rivers' flow – shall always justify itself before their pontifying rules. Thus are we building bridges that link only calculated differences; bridges that forbid us any freedom beyond the meticulous plans thought up by their architects. This is why our bridges are solid and efficient, they are made of terrible, rigid truths beyond which and under which it is dangerous to go without authorisation, but thanks to which, they say, world **PEACE** and stability are secured.

World citizens have created a New World, a new nature that comes from archaic Nature, but where each of us is a **SLAVE** of bridges and viaducts, a captive of this mandatory connexion that links all to all so that all be known to all. Man's sickly sweet lukewarmness has prohibited bridgeless shores. This man of cities has declared that, from now on, the unreachable is anathema, and this is why he hunts down the *incognito* as if it was the devil himself. To refuse the pontificate of **ASSEMBLED**, interlinked and ecclesiastical **HUMANITY**, is to challenge her truth and her sacredness, her divine character, and that is the greatest of all crimes: « Woe to the bridge breakers! Woe to the God who walks on water! », says the pontifying thinker. « Vanity, answers the God, I do not obey pontiffs. I have no need of bridges to reach the one I love and to know my neighbour! » And indeed, the river that separates all beings will one day be an infinite abyss, it will be infinity itself; not a single of our immutable truths will ever be able to cross such a space, no construction will ever bridge it. We must not build bridges, we must learn to walk on water! The Being must be able to walk on the endless horizon that separates him from his neighbour; the two must be able to meet by themselves, they must be able to be in communion without depending on an eternal truth which would link them. We must love without being forced to it by a sacred alliance, **WITHOUT THE VIADUCT OF A COMMANDMENT**. « Because I want it, because you want it, because we love each other freely »; thus will speak those who one day will walk on top of waters. — Such is one of the hidden meanings and one among the most beautiful acts that Christ did here below when he walked upon the water... on an hour's distance.

I - SONS OF MAN

The Four Hearts

The parable of the Sower or One man's progress

LUKE 8⁵⁻⁸

⁵ A sower went out to sow his seed: and as he sowed, some fell by the way side; and it was trodden down, and the fowls of the air devoured it. ⁶ And some fell upon a rock; and as soon as it was sprung up, it withered away, because it lacked moisture. ⁷ And some fell among thorns; and the thorns sprang up with it, and choked it. ⁸ And other fell on good ground, and sprang up, and bare fruit an hundredfold.

THE WAY, THE ROCKS, THE BUSHES AND THE HUMUS. Every reader of the *parable of the Sower* will easily identify the four grounds where the sower's seed is sowed. Commentators all agree to say that Christ here evokes four types of people, four different categories of listeners. However, I like to see in this story one and one listener only. The four grounds are actually the four hearts of a man — of **one and the same man**.

1 · THE WAY: *SEED IS TRODDEN DOWN BY PASSERS-BY AND EATEN BY BIRDS*

The first ground where the seed falls is, **by any human standard**, the most spiritual one. It is made of black asphalt, very even, smooth and clean, shiny and pure, consciously elaborated and high-tech. That first soil, boulevard-like, is the position of a man who is perfectly supervised by a most highly moral code of conduct. The asphalt of Laws is poured in that first heart and draws a road on which the *homo sapiens* does his best to spread out all his glory. This is the heart of the religious man, of the wiseman, where the gods of Torah work together with the gods of atheism and humanism. Those deities, avatars of pure Reason, hover above the earth as they run our reality through their unbendable laws. This is why, when the Gospel is sowed in such a heart, the winged-Beings of scientific and religious Logic immediately come to rob the seed and take it away. « What on earth is this clown who dares challenge our authority? » ask the majestic fowls. So do they remove the seed from that man's heart, because they are its masters. According to them, the Gospel is a much too silly and archaic discourse to be planted in the eminence of a heart they advanced by injecting high knowledge in it. Any possibility to leave the high road is then taken away from that man. That is, any possibility to step in doubt — to step in Faith.

What the gods aren't aware of is that the seed of the Gospel is, at the start, a fire thrown into the heart. It is in truth **a plough** beginning a strange work: it turns a man's heart over, ploughing through it, inciting it to contest the moral and scientific laws which rule over it. Little by little, the Sower wants to lead the individual man towards Another world. Over there, gods and truths have reverted to their serving position.

2 · THE ROCKS: *SEED SPRINGS UP SOON BUT, LACKING SOIL, WITHERS AWAY THE NEXT MOMENT*

In this context will arise a tragedy, a trial, a fall of some sort or another. That stifling heat of doubt, against which the individual man had conscientiously tried to protect himself, is yet occurring. Misfortune affects our man and he is overwhelmed by despair. Now, as he leaves the concrete road of the beginning, he enters his **second heart**. There, looking for solutions, he strays from the wisemen's road and dares to reach to the rocky places of a world clearly less conformist and less systematic. It is there, in that new place of enthusiasm that he suddenly sees the evangelical seed crack open in him. It brings him **hope** in the midst of the turmoil that has just hit him – the hope of an extraordinary way out of trial. On his knees, hands outstretched toward heaven, crying, singing and praising God, our man here is right in the middle of the second type of ground: he is in the process of opening his second heart.

Now the Gospel has just been growing to an almost technological speed that recalls the construction of the first road our man, however, thinks he has left for good. What kind of Gospel, then, is this? It is the Gospel of the artifice, of immediacy, the Gospel of the kind of faith that wants **to see in order to believe** — a faith, therefore, that is not faith. This is the Gospel that bears no hardship. It is precisely for this reason that it was rewritten to become a sort of anti-hardship charm. But of course reality and its trials do not back off before illusions or other amulets, even though these would be given the noble name of the Nazarene! The circumstances' stifling heat is in no way impressed nor disturbed by a blooming *truth* which is but a pseudo-revelation. Much the opposite. In the face of disillusion, powerlessness and failed hopes, and as belief evaporates under the heat, the furnace will then be doubly felt by our man. In no time at all, the great enthusiasm for the Extraordinary will burn out. This blissful heart's spirituality will dry on the spot even faster than it had grown.

3 · THE BUSHES: *SEED FALLS IN THE MIDDLE OF THORNS CHOKING THEIR GERMINATION*

At this stage, what is our man to do? Either he will return onto the asphalt ribbon, secure and comfortable – onto the first land and into his first heart – more or less enriched by the trial and vaguely ashamed of an episode he will see as eccentric. Or he will persevere and reach his **third heart**, which is also the third type of soil.

Thus ploughs on the plough of the Gospel. After it turned over the tar, the seed found stones, indeed, but it also found a little bit of soil where growth had succeeded in making a small breakthrough. From now on, the sower's ploughshare is tracing deeper furrows in the heart and it discovers much more loose soil in it where seed may be deposited. Unfortunately, that soil is still too close to the first road, it still is too much influenced and contaminated by the technology of the road workers of Morals, of scientific order, of that monotheism vociferating its laws of good and evil. That ground, that heart still hopes to turn the Sower into a King of this world: the third heart also demands that the sowed word give out immediate results, and give earthly happiness as proof for the All-Might. Unable to see that which the Gospel leads him to, our man therefore remains in deep concern for this world, for his own security and for his own prosperity – in short, for his Ego.

In the course of that third stage, whereas belief seems to find more root and moist to grow and develop, the commonest attitude of man is the following: he will build a church, a synagogue, a mosque, a university... and change the world! Much more. Thorny bushes will be transformed into religious flowers and wreaths to adorn civilisation, as man offers himself **to serve Society**. That is to say he will be working at embellishing the first ground's asphalt, he will try to please the first heart, to receive from it and with it the goods that the land of Civilised men can bestow. He will build a Messiah that is commensurate with man, an idol really, a God that can be venerated without travelling over to the land of the impossible, meaning, without having to find **a new heart** – that of the fourth ground.

Everything, then, has come full circle. The man in the parable is going round and round in circles around his three hearts. This trilogy makes up an optical illusion in which each heart is in the service of the other to simulate an impression of Progress. Through a certain course, at times antagonistic at other times collaborative, it all makes up a coherent and complementary whole, bringing about the well-known process of man's **positive evolution**. The first three hearts of *the parable of the Sower* are one and the same heart, that of the « earthy man », that of the *homo-sapiens* for whom the fourth heart remains unattainable – this one last ground of the parable where live the men who have broken their hearts of clay — who have smashed the *Adam*.

4 · THE HUMUS: *SEED FINDS A WELL-PREPARED AND RICH SOIL AND HARVEST IS PLENTIFUL*

This is the *not-yet-here-earth*. Here below, that soil is incognito, it's a *land-from-over-there*. It is the Other-man and it is a miracle — it is that coming harvest, hidden in Resurrection and hardly perceptible in our reality.

The fourth ground of *the parable of the Sower* is another identity. It is the nature that proceeds from the *Son of man*. This is the very nature that has seen the « No » of the Gospel **ploughing through all human possibilities**. To the man of Faith, that fourth soil is his true heart, whereas the other three are a permanent temptation to turn Christ into a reasonable and logical being, a temptation to turn Him into a co-builder of those eternal truths ruling our reality here below in such an inhumane manner. Thus the man of Faith, from the depths of his fourth heart, is engaged into a merciless fight against the return of everything religious, dogmatic or ecclesiastical, against the three hearts of the « earthy man » that still lie within him. The fruit he bears in that fight is that authentic spirituality **wholly given by the Sower**. An invisible fruit that no scales can weigh nor ruler can measure. That particular fruit shall be uncovered *after death*, for it is not about obedience nor good deeds nor virtues, but it is all about the impossible of Resurrection.

German poet R. M. RILKE – though he loathed official Christianity – wrote these words somewhere in his letters about his task as a poet. According to him, this task was about « *conveying to man the familiarity death has with the deepest joys and splendors of life* ». He declared that death was « **party to all that which lives.** »

Such is the actual meaning of *the parable of the Sower* — The Sower *went out to sow his seed...* and all along that incomprehensible work, he confidently, and without scruples, ruins the logical collusion between life and death. What is he aiming at? He is aiming at ploughing through your hearts. What is his goal? His goal is to kill you! For that reason says He also, « I am the Resurrection and the Life », as he came to put *man* to death and to beget the *son of man*. Indeed, the fourth ground is that land of Resurrection which, here below, can only be grasped in the incognito. It is this extraordinary **identity** towards which Christ leads the one who loves him... by opening the red sea before him! That is to say, by allowing him to **go beyond** both Life and Death, of course... but more importantly, beyond the eternal truths of the great-One, and of reason — those gods who still ordain with an iron fist, in our world, the two Titans on earth (Life *&* Death).

The four grounds of *the parable of the Sower* are truly a one and only heart. They stand for the advance of a man whose « earthy » hearts the Spirit is working to break so as to uncover the impossible heart of flesh God wants to give him. And if today you are standing at the far end of all your grounds, it may be that Christ is in the course of ushering you in the impossible of that new life, of that fourth heart, of that new being that in truth you are and that he will resurrect one day, this heart that will be full of living water one day and full of the **infinite possibilities**[1]... Can you see its horizon yet? Can you breathe its fragrance? If, like me, you take great delight in that air, if you too enjoy to be immersed in the darkness of Faith, hoping heavens will give you to persevere in that momentum until the end... then we probably are **brothers**, united through that strange existential work of the Spirit. In such a brotherhood, you do understand it, there is no more Church, as it lies among the thorns and on the tarred roads of the sociable and educated people. In such a brotherhood, you do understand it now, all are akklesiastical.

---

1 To quote KIERKEGAARD.

What seek ye?
Based on John 1$^{35\text{-}39}$

JOHN 1$^{35\text{-}39}$

^{35} Again the next day after John stood, and two of his disciples; ^{36} And looking upon Jesus as he walked, he saith, Behold the Lamb of God! ^{37} And the two disciples heard him speak, and they followed Jesus. ^{38} Then Jesus turned, and saw them following, and saith unto them, **What seek ye?** They said unto him, Rabbi (which is to say, being interpreted, Master,) **where dwellest thou?** ^{39} He saith unto them, Come and see. They came and saw where he dwelt, and abode with him that day: for it was about the tenth hour.

« WHAT SEEK YE? » are the **FIRST** words by Christ that John voices in his Gospel. They are the words of the beginning.

What an odd thing to write, really. Well! Isn't the Gospel supposed to recall an event that forever left its imprint on humankind? In the face of such a challenge, the narrative of that first meeting between the two apostles-to-be and the so-called Son of God sounds rather clumsy and inappropriate. With his « *What seek ye?*», isn't John completely beside the messianic perspective he wants to demonstrate? A **TRUTH** like this one, should it not make its entrance in our lives crowned with sublime and wonder, exalting the mysteries of a superior theology? And above all, should not this truth be utterly pragmatic, to the point of bestowing goodness to every fibre of humankind?

This is how a religious man naturally follows and hears Christ – like someone who has discovered a treasure, clings to it like a leech and hurries for the loot. The conversations which take place between traditional Christianity and the Nazarene have **NOTHING IN COMMON** anymore with that first evangelical dialogue! Now good Christians sit lined up like toy soldiers, dumb and quiet before their Master's chair, mindful to take down notes of some *spiritual* knowledge, because they know acquiring such a knowledge will allow them to be first. On the opposite side, those belonging to a less intellectual strand of Christianity will prefer to use their bodies. That sort of Christians get drunk with enthusiasm or hysteria, shaking at the feet of their prophetic and mystic stars. In this type of place, everyone is happy to catch a few golden coins of the divine, foolishly thinking those « Christian amulets » will resolve all of their everyday problems.

However, John is making no mistake as he drops his enigmatic « *What seek ye?* » where nobody expects it. And when he avoids the traditional image of the empty vase the divine potter needs to fill, he does so with an eye to leading us to some other place. He simply leads us close to that particular manner the ancient prophets had to approach the truth, a skill he is familiar with from an early age, since Judaism had been practicing it from early on under the name of *mahloket*. That is, a controversy, a discussion – a **BREAK**, in fact. With this practice, seeking God is no more about taking that treasure we first imagine even before we can discover it. It is on the contrary about breaking that image of the divine we make for ourselves – **WE MUST BREAK THE IDOL**. The seeker must no more be filling his earthly vase with a *mystico-divine energy*, via theology or mystical experience, but he must break it and lose it. And if, through that breaking, another vase is resurrected, that one then will have no need to be filled with God! The distinctive feature of that new nature is precisely to be a divine one, to be made of **ANOTHER** nature. Seeking the son of man, it is in the first place learning to kill the man, it is learning to severely question him. It is learning to doubt. A faith that does not know the hammer of doubt is but a fable for children.

This is why Christ, that same one John just called « rabbi », which is to say, being interpreted, « *Master* », began his very short earthly peregrination by a **QUESTION**, by a first breaking. A question that is almost a rejection, bordering on non-invitation and turning down. As for the two men to whom it is asked, they will need to prove they are not some *toy soldier students* or some *miracle hunters* whose critical faculty has gone missing. They are doing just so when they, in turn, answer by another **QUESTION**, « Where dwellest thou? » Which is to say, « Who are you? » Is it not the most beautiful of all questions one could ask God while yet being in his presence? This is the very question which sets as a basic rule that everything I prejudge, everything I see with supporting evidence, everything I conceive about His person precisely needs to be questioned and put in doubt.

Therein lies true nobility. It is this attitude which eventually prompted Christ to invite them, « Come and see where I dwell; come, and I'll tell you who I am. » The two disciples finally spent their whole lives discovering who the Nazarene was and where he was from. One does not meet God with mystical thrills and dogmatic truths.

« What seek ye? » — For truth looters who mass together around an idol of Christ, those first words are but a statement of the obvious, a little naive. « Gosh! will they say, just like God, we are seeking justice, happiness and success down here, that's why we're his legitimate sons. » On hearing such an answer, Christ would probably have sent these men back to Moses or to some other tables of eternal laws, failing to see in them that noble feature with which the Spirit breaks the eternal dogmas of self-evident truths. Indeed, the Moses of humankind and their disciples: are they not the ones who, since forever, are endlessly discussing to elaborate laws, to discover new truths which they extract from logical knowledge? Are they not the **STAUNCH SUPPORTERS** of a World which, they think, sends them in order to purify it — as wise men and politicians will say; to sanctify it, as Christianity will say; to repair it, as Judaism will say; to deliver it from its wishes and desires, as Buddhism will say. And despite all their talks on the « salvation of the soul » and on the « soul of the world » this gang of dogmatic smooth talkers cling to their earthly well-being like a flea to the neck of the dog that shelters it. The infinity of another place and of another nature is to them but a distant and dangerous tale. To declare that it is possible for us to exit this present and finite place, this present finite nature – all this is, at the bottom of their hearts, only a utopia humankind must be cured of. They believe it is the price to pay for men to be able to follow on their glorious march towards Progress.

« What seek ye? » — For anyone seizing it, the whole Gospel lies in these founding words. Just like the first seekers, we must ask ourselves « **WHERE DWELLS** » the truth, for the fact is, it does not dwell among us and it is very little mindful of the earthly well-being barbarians and wise men alike are addicted to. And when Christ answers men, « Come and see where I dwell », how well does he know that very few will follow him. He knows how much Truth is a nightmare to them, the truth whose « kingdom is not of this world nor this city ». The truth which, here below, has « no place to lay its head ». It is to the desert that Christ leads those who are seeking him, and it is in the desert that **HE PREPARES AND LEVELS A PATH FOR THEM** into the world-to-come. This is the place where a few ones still follow him today, this is where they dwell and stay with him « all the day » of their lives. And for these few ones, to not being heard by « the city » (society) – a city which no longer seeks an Unknown Somewhere Else while yet plundering these few ones, in the premonition of its coming defeat — that has become something they cannot get used to. A deep sadness.

The popes
Pontifex Maximus

Pope John Paul II declared in a memorandum that «faith and **reason** are like two wings on which the human spirit rises to the contemplation of truth.[1]» Lev Shestov had a quite different stance on the subject. Indeed, considering the ancient narrative of Genesis, the Russian philosopher was thus speaking, «For reason is the fiery sword by means of which the Angel placed by God at the gates of Paradise drives men away.[2]» He was referring to the heavenly beings evoked in the biblical text, «and he placed at the east of the garden of Eden Cherubims, and a flaming sword which turned every way, to keep the way of the tree of life.» (Gen 3^{24})

Who are we to believe? The theology of the prestigious Supreme Pontiff who ruled in Vatican for nearly thirty years, or a barely known philosopher who went into exile to Paris where he died? For one, Reason raises man, for the other, Reason deprives man of the greatest good. The Pope takes off with Reason to meet divine truth whereas Shestov sees in Reason an unbendable enemy constantly threatening him. How then, from the same biblical text, could such an abyss

---

[1] John Paul II, *Fides et Ratio* · Encyclical, 14 September 1998.
[2] Lev Shestov, *Potestas Clavium*, «On the Roots of Things.»

form between those men? Do we see mankind dividing itself up equally between its two sides? Niet! All men have long agreed with the popes' views – or rather, it is Rome who long ago joined intelligent and *reasonable* men!

In the same encyclical, JOHN PAUL II gets into deeper water as he eventually adds, « philosophical thought is often the only ground for understanding and dialogue with those who do not share our faith ». Let it be reminded that the Roman Bishop bears a title inherited from Latin Antiquity, a title which used to indicate the highest priest of **PAGAN ROME** – the *Pontifex Maximus*, that is, the Great Bridge Builder. JOHN PAUL II, in the tradition of his multiple predecessors, is building in this instance a philosophical bridge in order to unite the Church with the rest of reasonable mankind. This way, Christian men will see in Reason one of the spirit's wings that allows men to rise and fly from progress to progress. It then belongs to each of us to decide what suits them best as a second wing – *Science*, goes the Atheist; *Theology*, popes will say, pretending it is the « Science of Faith ». This is how the fire of Reason has burned Faith and then turned it into a divine science. The popes took the spirit's liberty and transformed it into a fiery and vindictive sword; they tore up its wings. They do not fly, they walk on earth, burning everything that does not obey their reason – like that Failed-man, *the sinner*.

SHESTOV, however, had undertaken the task, « not to reconcile science and philosophy but to sunder them ». He adds, « the deeper and more bitter the enmity between philosophy and science, the more humanity will win by it[3] ».

---

3 LEV SHESTOV, *In Job's Balances*, « On the Philosophy of History. »

As for himself, he smashed the bridge built by the popes. He remained there, exiled from the other side of the abyss, joining with the small remnant of men for whom that knowledge possessed by the Angel with the fiery sword is but magic for the intelligent. What sort of philosophy free from the logical workings of Reason did SHESTOV elaborate this side of the chasm? The one, he declared, that « proposes not to accept but to overcome the self-evidences and which introduces into our thought a new dimension – **FAITH**. »

And so the popes threw out faith to Reason, that fascinates them, and turning it into a Science of God, they built up cathedrals of rules and doctrines to which one only needs to bow down and to obey in order to reach the divine. But one does not buy Faith with the lights of Reason and its wise moral. And not only does Faith **DISOBEY** Reason, but furthermore, it wants to subject it to Freedom because it knows how Reason goes crazy when in a ruling position. Faith in God feeds on a liberty that no logic can catch hold of. Therefore, whoever builds a bridge in order to tie them one to another is actually performing a transplant, on the same body, of feathers of divine Freedom next to the leaden wing of reasonable truths. In so doing, they are preparing the world to collapse into the bottomless abyss that precisely separates God from our Sciences of the truth.

The kingdom of God, where faith leads to, is a place where truths no longer accuse the soul with their fiery swords. There, the angelic fire of their power has lost the authority their self-evident truths still wield down here. In divine reality, truths live and die at the discretion of *the sons of man*'s will. There, their contradictions do not trouble neither beings nor nature. This is why, in the present world, a man of faith will be tense with all of his strength in the resistance against the popes of wisdom. For he refuses, lest he associate with them, to burn those budding wings his God forms him to go meet Him one day. It happened during those painful wanderings that SHESTOV came upon the following consolation – he was then remembering « the battle against self-evident truths » that Christ also waged when He was tempted in the wilderness:

> When Athens proclaims *urbi et orbi*, for the city and for the world: ***If you wish to subject everything to yourself, subject yourself to reason,***[4] Jerusalem hears through these words: ***All these things will I give thee if thou wilt fall down and worship me***; and answers: ***Get thee hence, Satan! For it is written: Thou shalt worship the Lord thy God and Him only shalt thou serve.***[5]

---

4 SENECA, *Letters to Lucilius*, letter 37-4 (Latin in original: *Si vis tibi omnia subjicere, te subjice rationi*).

5 LEV SHESTOV, *Athens and Jerusalem*, « On the Philosophy of the Middles Ages. »

The Untamable Samson
A reading of the Book of Judges

ON THE BOOK OF JUDGES

WE ARE DEALING WITH SAMSON'S STORY somehow like we would with an egg out of boiling water – it is impossible to keep it in the palm of our hand, we have to pass it on to our neighbour or let it spoil on the floor for fear of burning. Of course the smartest solution is to dip it in cold water, then we can peel it and use it at our convenience. This is the way scholars interpret the book of Judges, in a manner that seems very plausible[1]. Here is a summary of their theory: the figure of Samson is used as a religious and political pretext, and so are his fellow judges. The Chronicles of Judges are actually an indictment of their methods since their efficiency does not last beyond the lifespan of each of the staged leaders.

The goal of these stories which recount their short-lived achievements is to discreetly eulogize the coming establishment of the kings of Judah and to introduce them as being the timely solution. The judges herald these kings through their failure at stabilising the nation once and for all. Some

---

1 See among others ISABELLE DE CASTELBAJAC, Israel's Judges: A Deuteronomistic Invention? *Revue de l'Histoire des religions* n°221.

author or group of authors who lived after the facts (under King Josiah or after returning from Babylon) probably recovered some historical base they have reworked, thereby giving their contemporaries evidence that the historical birth of the Judah monarchy was in God's plans. This discourse tends to say that Israel's history at the time of Judges was floundering because the moral alliance did not have absolute priority among the people. This is how the coming monarchy stemming from Judah was given legitimacy as the only one capable of restoring the Torah alliance and of gathering the tribes back around the Jerusalem Temple for, says the author, « In those days there was no king in Israel, but every man did that which was right in his own eyes. » (17^6 and 21^{25})

The figure of Samson easily fits this theory. His wild impulsiveness, his insubordination and his naive approach of women seem to stamp him as a morally disapproved person. Moreover, his family, coming from Dan's tribe, live in Tsorea, on a rocky crest at the border between Judah and the Philistine cities in the valley. Dan's tribe, we can read, « sought them an inheritance to dwell in: for unto that day all their inheritance had not fallen unto them among the tribes of Israel » (18^1). With this biographical data, Samson is naturally standing at the border between two lands: the ancient mythology, more or less nomadic, which would be soon absorbed by the more efficient and more « modern » civilisation slowly germinating that the coming Judah monarchy offers to embody. This is why men of that tribe will give Samson up to the Philistines ($15^{11\text{-}13}$), thus disowning the ancient ways of the Danites they deemed obsolete. In the end, and as a result of the events linked to that last judge, the author recounts the Danites' migration northwards and the falling apart of their conduct (18). This is how the book of Judges ends – the Davidic monarchy, hand in hand with its legal magistrature flanking priests and prophets are knocking at the door!

In a more distant future, beyond the sole book of Judges, this ideology hoists the banner of a policy that is Democratic and Fair. Of course its messianic characteristic has been preserved all along, under various terms, as a justification for its inescapable advent. Century by century monarchies will be transforming into the great administrative democracies we know today, where religious men become moral educators, prophets become experts in truth certificates and the whole of them unite at last to civilise the world and bring peace to the people they are sent to teach. In this new context, this leading clique slyly replace the elusive faith of the Samsons with a clause of *moral and intellectual responsibility*. And in order to prevent any deviation, they stir the roaring of crises and the threats of anarchy's hoodlums. Artists are called upon for the task. To all from a younger age, they tell crafty tales of those pathetic heroes from Antiquity, of their underdeveloped centuries during which, « there was no civilised nation, and where every man did that which was right in his own eyes. »

Paradoxically, scholars have done a great favour to Faith when they made a breach in the Old Testament's historical credibility, when they put on the foreground its mixture of fiction and reality, and when they declared that « the biblical historiography was first and foremost written to forge the present and to convey an ideological message[2] ». Because if Bible disparagers are at first proud of their conclusions which are protected by the data of archeology and modern history, they eventually force a laugh when they see the trap in which they have fallen! For, as they unveil the text's costume, they consequently transfer all the attention on its background. And this ideology precisely tends to « separate History from myth in the name of morality », Isabelle de Castelbajac explains. She shows that « the collapse of authority has its cause in the withdrawal of the law », and that the solution is to be found in « the establishing of a code of good conduct and in giving those who lead human affairs the sense of responsibility. » This is exactly the sort of message a modern man will advocate when he is supporting Democracy while scorning the Bible! From then on such a man is faced with a paradox. His scholarly lights on the biblical corpus have eventually unveiled, in the very midst of the enemy he vilifies, the reflection of his own face. His enemy is actually one of the matrixes he comes from! Consequently, his biblical criticism really served his humanistic ideal but at the same time it deceived him. The very essence of his ideal – an ideal which proclaims a golden age – could already be found in the biblical text! As modern man arrogantly examines and puts on trial the words of the ancient, he is unable to see that he will end up finding himself in them.

But does it suffice to put the Old Testament in the cold water of scholars to solve what it says for good? Must we put the book back on the shelf and rest assured we have

---

2 See Nadav Na'aman, The Bible at the crossroads of the sources, *Annales: Histoire, Sciences Sociales*, n°6, 2003.

completely elucidated it because the learned show us the O.T. took historical facts hostage in order to justify a modern ideology? Rather, is it not memory, albeit rearranged, that takes us hostage as we stop our thinking here? As we transcribe it at our convenience and according to the angle from which we observe it? Quite evidently, Samson's story was told precisely thanks to the care of ideologues who, like us, thought they were masters of the past and builders of modernity. In fact, History deceives wise men by making them believe it is dead. As they decipher tombstones from the past with their epitaphs, convinced they are reaching THE truth where the main point will soon be said, they are, on the contrary and from generation to generation, assisting in making abound this message of the past. And so this is how scholars read stones and then fall asleep — when others are using their work to go and lift stones, so as to hear the truth singing! For the latter, enigmatic History has come alive and it reveals the scraps of some hidden and invisible meaning, not looking towards the past but towards a distant future to-come. Ideologues examine, weigh, measure, and dress the corpses of History, and with these corpses they clothe the present and leave to others the care to hunt for the *second path*[3] and to clad what lies beyond tombstones.

---

3 « Revelations are not given to man to make the life of man easier or to transform stones into bread; neither to change the course of history. History knows only one course, from the past, through the present, direct into the future; but revelation presupposes some second path. » Lev Shestov, *Revelations of Death*, The Conquest of the Self-Evident (Dostoevsky's Philosophy), chap. 14.

THE BEGINNING

Samson is the one who « shall begin to deliver Israel out of the hand of the Philistines », an angel announced to his parents (13[5]). But he failed. A failure, as explained earlier, which serves as a pretext to prove deliverance was to come from the Judean monarchy. This is why the tribe of Judah handed Samson over to the Philistines. And whoever would accuse the people from Judah of disowning an angel from God would be seriously wrong. Samson fell, the retort would be, because he did not respect the status of « consecrated » he had received. He was immoral, uncontrollable and wild. Deliverance requires to be achieved by a meticulous establishing of the moral Alliance in the entire public sphere, one would finally add – hence the need of a monarchy! The text always seems to fall back on its feet, in this case, those of the Torah and of the sacred Temple presented as being its source. Better still, the angel's message is thusly reworded, « Samson began to deliver Israel out of the hand of the Philistines, but he was not found worthy, so the angel handed the task over to the Judean monarchies which set up the mosaic Laws into a governmental system. » Thus was abolished the age of heroes and ushered in the age of politics.

This is a typically Greco-Roman way of thinking. Legendary Achilles, just like Samson, fills the crowds with enthusiasm and we are all pleased to enjoy his demigod title (and the mane of hair, for Samson), while he fights heroically on the side of the Greek armies in the Trojan war. But when he deserts the army, full of anger against King Agamemnon over beautiful Briseis, he then becomes unworthy. The lad is not reliable, he is fickle. His whims are controlling him so much that he is unable to feed the people and to hold an international office. Incidentally, many researchers censure « Homer's heroes for being especially prone to violent and quick mood shifts, to suffer from mental instability[4] ». The sceptre will be preferably handed to the Emperor-philosopher Marcus Aurelius, a fervent Stoic, keeper of ethics and accuser of passions. Let him wage war as he pleases, let him expand the Empire or let him defend it tooth and nail, like he actually did, but let him remain human and not be an uncontrollable demigod, else his *Achille's heel* shall be stricken, his mane of hair cut and his glory withered. He will be made to fall! A man anointed by God is therefore, in this perspective, one whose human behaviour is normal and balanced. If that is not the case, he will be diagnosed with some psychological or demonic disorder, very often a bit of both. So today, no biblical prophet nor even Christ would be given a different treatment than they got when they were living. Those who honour their graves are precisely the most vehement as, to them, the thought that the prophets might be « abnormal » is a terrible nightmare.

What has Samson « begun »? Of what deliverance is he the beginning? Precisely that which is impossible; that from the obstacle of difference, that is, the hand of the strange stranger. Such a deliverance is impossible in the real world. There will always be some Other coming from some *other* land or from across the seas, with *other* gods and *other* customs. There will always be a hand of Philistine, some other *truth* claiming to be truer than mine, therefore threatening my blessing, my territory, my wealth, the future that some god

---

[4] NILSSON, quoted by E. R. DODDS, *The Greeks and the Irrational*, chapter I.

has promised me on the land of my fathers. The obliteration of that Other can only be conceived through ecumenism, that is to say, by having everything «come live together» under a single-One concept. By going from the Other to the single-One, from God to the diabolical! Union on the whole inhabited earth, either that of a total policy or that of ecumenism – those are merely the two faces of a same coin called hell. It means forcing everyone to submit their particular concept to a Ruling-concept, it means putting to death the pretention to escape it that every one has a right to. The only solution which would save us from seeing the Other as an enemy would be – to be free from every concept and every truth. It is our immersion in conceptual truths which turns difference into rivalry. The enemy is not the other, the enemy is any idea of a general truth, a concept taken to its logical extreme in ecumenism. Accordingly, to be saved from the hand of difference is a utopia in the midst of our reality. Samson is a utopian to whom realism must be opposed: an earthly kingdom ruled by universal laws! It will be the age of politics and of their mass slaughters; it will be the disappearance of ancient heroes whose freedom is a dream to the hearts of children. It will be the age of the moderns and of its normal people, psychiatric cases sick from having killed utopia.

What strikes us in Samson is his freedom and his independence, reflected by a spirituality which seems «too simple» to be true. Samson does not burden himself with organised rituals, liturgy or holocausts. He speaks to God spontaneously, with no religious prop. In the same way he rather seems to act instinctively and to abide to no justifying code. Furthermore, living at the border between Judah and the Philistines, he has one foot in the Israel ideology whose consecrated land reclaims a policy, and the other foot with the Danites who are still looking for a place to settle. It follows that the otherness of the Philistine is not that strange to him. This is why his activity starts on that border, where his liberty to embrace difference is natural to him, although it may be provoking to others (14^{10}). Samson makes his announcement at a wedding banquet: he, the Danite, is going to marry a Philistine woman!

So as to quash the budding conflict, Samson engages in an intellectual and instructive process, using a playful tone. He proposes the riddle of the lion and honey (14^{14}) he has drawn from his own prophetic experience. The « thirty sheets and thirty change of garments » he gambles stand for the abundance of human glories, that is to say the skills and knowledge with which civilisations clothe reality and provide for their earthly needs. However, due to the fact that the proposed riddle is inspired, it is unsolvable through those skills we exert in order to dominate life. Samson teaches with a parable: our wisdoms, our riches and our joys cannot reach the divine treasures where differences unite. Although they have the strength and the kingship of a lion they do not give God's mysterious honey. As he defeats the wisdom of the guests, Samson gives them in the end the opportunity to bring him in dowry the « thirty sheets and thirty change of garments », meaning, to approve his marriage, to seal a union they anticipate as an impossible one — and this way, to shut the door on the natural conflict between opposed truths, in this case, the Philistine's and the Israelite's.

Of course the Philistine camp will not be humble enough to acknowledge Samson's inspiration. On the contrary, behaving like foxes, they will steal the riddle's answer by threatening the bride. To be sure, they will obtain the prize the Danite has promised, but they will harvest his wrath together with it as thirty Philistines from a neighbouring town provide for the garments at the cost of their lives. Samson's wrath is certainly not to be emulated but it is neither there as a reproach for a supposed unbalanced nature. It serves to say that the inflexible law remains the only standard applied to any one who has dismissed faith in the impossible as if that faith was a fable or a game. As for the Israelite camp, Samson's comrades who had come with him, these will keep quiet. Witnessing the events, they will take advantage of the situation and betray him, as the beloved will be « stolen » by one of them, with her father's approval (14^{20}). Having cowardly benefited from the conflict between Samson and the Philistines without taking sides, they will see the truth of their actions rebound on them like a boomerang. For them also will the laws of reality be put into action: father, bride and thieves will be put to death (15^6).

THE FOXES

And so Samson is rejected after having been bitterly despoiled from both sides equally. From then on he is leaving the adolescence of his prophetic status. In this manner, along the way of his own progress, he will understand the whole depth of the riddle he had been carrying. Indeed he had closely reached it, but its most essential meaning had not yet been revealed to him. If the lion must die so that the honey be given... — Had not the angel told Samson's mother, «For the child shall be a Nazarite to God from the womb to the day of his death» (13^7)? Which means that he himself must die in order to reveal what, in a man, must die.

For the time being Samson is still drinking contempt as he is more or less seen as a naive and impulsive man, which is how the popular mind portrayed him. He then embarks upon a direct action opposing both antagonistic forces that have united against him. He will target what is most precious to them – the actual economy of their wealth. By striking the economy of the Philistines he will expose that it is joint to that of the Judeans, and that the lives of both peoples are based on the same values. By this move he enters the adult age of his calling:

> And Samson went and caught three hundred foxes, and took firebrands, and turned tail to tail, and put a firebrand in the midst between two tails. And when he had set the brands on fire, he let them go in the standing corn of the Philistines, and burnt up both the shocks, and also the standing corn, with the vineyards and olives. (15$^{4-5}$)

Samson has just officially turned into a public enemy. He is hunted from all sides to the point he has to take refuge in a cavern, on his own, where he will probably be living for some time. Besides not finding help with the Judeans nor rallying them around his vision, they turn him in to the Philistines. This is how they secure peace for themselves and protect their own economy threatened by retaliation. The first situation is then clearly confirmed: Samson's prophetic position is rejected by both Philistines and Judeans whose interests are common!

The tail to tail foxes are an image for the ambiguity of these so-called antagonistic ideologies, which actually use similar methods and strive towards the same goal – the Philistines and the Judeans both want to be the monarchy that will dominate the other. One and the other think they embody divine truth on earth. The Philistine and Israelite doctrines are therefore placed at the same level, tied together. And in a more modern context, so are those of the Western and Eastern worlds, or those of the religious and the atheists, capitalism and marxism, etc. They all fall into one category and, although at various degrees, their antagonism is only an illusion. Their conception of divine inspiration is only there to serve their interests, each according to their needs. Moreover they use it as a banner and a pretext. These doctrines set up religious and political systems where duties and prohibition abundantly thrive. They establish schools for the « consecrated » and theology institutes so as to put inspiration under their control. And so they become a subversion of the revelation, with varying degrees of sincerity and of spiritual awareness.

Samson's deed evokes the idea CHESTERTON will later put into words when speaking of « Christian virtues gone mad », meaning syncretism. In its incredulous haste to make the revelation a tangible reality, Christianity absorbed all the philosophical and cultic juices cherished by the societies where it settled. As for Samson, he is telling us about *the truth of the promised land gone mad.* From the moment that truth wanted to become flesh in the Judean Kingdom it signed compromises with its mighty neighbours and sealed them with the blood of the prophets. Judaism rejected Christ precisely for this reason – because its theologians saw as an indignity that the Truth might become flesh! Besides, Judaism rebukes Christ for his refusal to have his kingship become flesh, for his assertion that his kingdom will not be embodied here below in a people, that it is not of this world and that the promised land is the Kingdom of heaven only: there is neither Jew nor Greek anymore! This is why the Church and Judaism are also two foxes tied tail to tail, they use similar methods in order to dishonour their inspiration and they obey the same masters. Just like Samson's comrades, the Church despoils the revelation by calling herself a spouse, then she gives Christ over to the current ruling power. This is how she engages in prostitution with the political systems and the doctrines of the times and places she is crossing. Her hope is to see « Christian » values being imposed to the world through the Western civilisation she serves – Christian virtues « gone mad ».

In fact, the monarchy system that will come after the abolition of the inspired-judges is a sample of how our societies are being constructed. We set tail to tail different doctrines that are supposedly opposed, for instance, Judaism, Greco-Roman philosophies, ancient myths, or Christianity. Then we put in prison the inspired ones who are too inspired and who are endangering the human project. Believing is a commendable thing as long as it is only about caring for the poor, however, « living by faith » is condemnable from the moment a man gains too much freedom and independence out of it. And if that consecrated man remains firm and does not join the ekklesia, then some moral transgression or psychological anomaly will be found in him and it will shut his mouth. Because no one has the right to escape the community verdict and all must live by this law; upon it relies the universal empire in the making and its ecumenical religion.

Similarly, Samson's progress is an overview of the prophetic intention. The first level of understanding where fiction and reality intermingle actually hides a deep subtlety. On the border where he is standing, Samson reaches to the roots as he uncovers the common spirit that unites apparently conflicting ideologies, and his revelation works as a spark – it sets torches on fire. It unmasks the hypocrisy of such a system then drives it crazy, pushing it towards self-destruction. Because « antagonists need one another to perpetuate the discord that keeps them alive », RENÉ GIRARD explains, « their secret agreement aims at preventing the unveiling of their common truth, the truth whose emergence they feel would annihilate them simultaneously[5] »

THE FALL: DELILAH

Samson is now hated by all and he is handed over to the dominant power following his bold action with the foxes. He then inflicts his opponents another humiliating and crushing defeat as they try to arrest him (15^{15}). He has become truly free, but this time at the cost of solitude and a very painful wandering. An endless status quo settles in at the end of which he will be defeated by the fatigue of a situation that appears to be humanly unbearable. His fall into immorality is a fabrication by the author of the book of Judges who is looking for a way to disapprove the solitary Nazarite without

---

[5] RENÉ GIRARD, *The One by Whom Scandal Comes, Noble Savages and Others*, chap. 1, second part.

denying his calling. Delilah actually represents the prophet's languor as he is being put to the test over time. He is seeking consolation, recognition and communion. Who will understand him? With whom will he be able to open his heart without being rejected or betrayed? Samson has a hunger to love and be loved, he is hungry for the fellowship that has been constantly fleeing from him. Could it be that he was wrong? Have his opponents not seen clearly when they blamed him for being antisocial and over the top? Samson is suffering, lamenting, he is self-doubting; like prophet Jeremiah:

> Woe is me, my mother, that thou hast borne me a man of strife and a man of contention to the whole earth! (JER 15^{10})

and lastly, he is doubting God:

> I sat alone because of thy hand: for thou hast filled me with indignation. Why is my pain perpetual, and my wound incurable, which refuseth to be healed? wilt thou be altogether unto me as a liar, and as a water that fail? (JER 15$^{17b\text{-}18}$)

This is how he moderates himself and renews a dialogue with those who had been hunting him down for so long. Delilah is their ambassador in disguise. She will know, at the appropriate time, how to sway Samson's prophetism towards organised religion. She flatters him, suggesting his prophetic talents could secure him a prominent place and substantial profit within the established religion (16^5). However he still needs to accept being « tamed » as it is openly asked of him, « Tell me, I pray thee, wherein thy great strength lieth, and wherewith thou mightest be bound to afflict thee » (16^6).

Samson almost engages in psychoanalysis ahead of its time, the stakes being that he give up his wild strength to become civilised, which is to say fit to take an administrative religious office. He will give in, not by his free will, but pressed by that psychological force he had not known until then, for « his soul was vexed unto death » (16^{16}). In a word, he became depressive. It was the bitter fruit of his indecision taking root on the one hand, and of the constant accusation religious intelligence put on his back on the other hand. Having doubted his calling and sought a communion he knew was yet deceitful, he ends up exhausted and falls asleep in the lap of a false consolation. The ideology of a victorious people united around a Temple where dwells their god now rules over his tired and sleeping heart.

Sleep, for a prophet, means death. It means forsaking the anointing, in other words, it means the impossibility to see. Samson's eyes are put out. A long ordeal begins for him. True, he is brought to the front stage like a glorious trophy, he is applauded, he makes the delight of the elite and he leads worship services with skill, but his « LORD was departed from him »! He is shackled to a politico-religious system that no longer demands him to burn dogmas and traditions, but to grind them so as to make out of them a bread of servitude for men. Had he been a deceiver? In that case, he will live in peace under the people's anointing, with thirty garments and a well-filled wallet. But if he is a true prophet then his calling is irrevocable, because God loves faithfulness – he will bring him back to life by reviving his faith, a faith that no one can take from the divine hand.

RESURRECTION AND JUDGEMENT

When the religious lion dies, the divine honey may be flowing once again. The ultimate stage of the accomplished prophet is victory by defeat — this is the Messiah paradox: resurrection. We must die to earthly ideologies in order to resurrect, not unite them in some ecumenical compromise, but destroy them! Samson discovers the true meaning of the words upon which his calling was based, «He shall begin to deliver» (13^5). The enemy is not the Philistine stranger or the false Judean brother who betrayed him, or the absent Danite family, or the comrade who won the spouse, or the won spouse, etc. Samson is going to destroy the Temple by breaking its conquering pillars! The Temple symbolises community divinities and collective powers. Its pillars are the laws and the efficient truths men serve. Civilisations erect them like representations for their gods, for their certainties, their absolute truths. They take refuge in them, they worship them and go to war in their names. Any Temple is an idol, any community declaring itself to be the embodiment of truth is an idolater and any church aligning itself with it is an idol.

God does not dwell in a community, a truth or a Temple, but he dwells in the individual person. His presence does not increase when individuals add up but, on the contrary, it decreases: «As soon as there is a crowd, God becomes invisible» KIERKEGAARD said. The world of addition, which is that of communities, is the world of the Beast in which number holds the power. Therefore, Samson's destroying the Temple is a prophecy that announces Christ, «Destroy this temple, and in three days I will raise it up» (JOHN 2^{19}).

He was talking about his body, about his own death. Because only Christ has succeeded in breaking the pillars belonging to the temple of the most powerful collective truth – the lion of Death. It is man only he is calling to become a temple of God, a kingdom of God and a king.

« God only exists for the individual » wrote KIERKEGAARD in his *Journal*, and Samson, the individual man, was a temple by himself. Therefore he was sufficient to destroy the false temple of Judaism and of the Philistine religion. His death is not a prophecy for the Judean monarchy but for the destruction of all earthly kingdoms, all temples, all truths and all churches. Let each man now choose his death – like Samson, by pushing the pillars of the concepts imposed on him; or by suffering their collapse. And let the miserable man who still resists the tamer's whip take courage, Christ will soon burn that whip, break the last pillar of his grave, then he will crown him with hair like a mane.

Vashti the queen
To Christian women

ONLY VASHTI THE QUEEN brings a true spiritual quality to the Book of Esther proposed by the Old Testament. For the way God is depicted in this text is sickening, the depiction of woman and more generally of the couple is totally outrageous and as for poor Esther, if she was not a zealot she would share all of queen Jezebel's features: an ambitious female politician rigid in the extreme under her honeyed and very talented strategies. Without the presence of Vashti the queen, who is repudiated by the king at the very beginning of the story, there would be nothing in the narrative to give its content any spiritual value. But what is the most surprising about this book is how it was received by Christians: they have been blind to the point of seeing inspiration precisely where there is not any. Esther, who in the eyes of the author represents the Torah with its equally radiant and merciless justice, becomes in Christianity an image for the Church, victorious and thriving on earth. King Ahasuerus, however, remains for both the image of God, and uncle Mordecai represents the Messiah-King: a man just to excess and nonetheless an incredibly efficient man of war.

The book's structure is almost childish and as silly as can be, and there certainly lies its efficiency, considering that men do not like to be asked *men*'s questions. Therefore this text fails to lift us with any paradox but instead it bombards us with stereotypes and obvious truths at almost every sentence; it is a story in the best tradition of today's Bollywood fictions.

God's chosen people (Jews for ones, Christians for the others) are meant to receive **earthly domination** on all Nations. But here comes a sardonic and wily enemy, impersonated by Haman (the Devil), who succeeds in deceiving the king (God) and organising the extermination of the people of the « saints ». But, coup de théâtre! Most holy virgin and orphan Esther will consent, for a good cause, to share the king's bed – understand here that only the Torah or the Church have a genuine intimacy with God. Out of this connivance with the god, depicted under the odd features of a king forcing a woman to get into his bed, will arise deliverance. Esther, who became queen by her charms, which delighted a jaded king – understand, by her obedience and here smooth docility – will eventually save her people at the very last moment. However not without help from the very pure Mordecai, a man of integrity not to say a fundamentalist, ready to give himself as a suicide martyr in order to destroy vile Haman. All's well that ends well. The feeble and ingenuous king, who did not even once work up a sweat except in palace pleasures, finally hands over the key of royal authority to Esther and Mordecai. All in all, the book of Esther exhales a strong koranic smell.

Indeed, take note that all this did require no less than a bloodbath in the whole kingdom. The chosen people, gone on a crusade and armed by the king (God), made short of their ennemies. Moreover and as if that was not enough, Queen Esther outdid herself when her second petition to the king is again granted to her: the kingdom's inhabitants were thus treated to an extension of the bloodbath, as she requested an extra day of war to exterminate the bad ones up to the last (cf. 9^{13}). Esther is perfect. She is as inflexible as cruel, and like Jezebel who knew how to proclaim fasts (1 Kings 21^9) and organise wars, Esther used the whole variety of her gifts to administer the people and supervise them according to a religious way of life which was as conquering as immutable: « And the decree of Esther confirmed these matters of Purim; and it was written in the book » (9^{32}).

Esther is the **anti-Shulamite**. The Shulamite is that spiritual woman filled with freedom introduced in the Song of Songs. Vashti the queen however foreshadows her, as a sort of herald. Unintendedly, the author is telling us something there at last! Vashti, like the Shulamite, cannot stand the objectification she is imposed on; she also wants the power to choose her life as she intends it. She too therefore will irritate the establishment which in turn will reject her — so does declare the Shulamite in the Song: « My mother's children were angry with me; they made me the keeper of the vineyards [...] My vineyard, which is mine, is before me » (1^6 & 8^{12}). Her people had likewise forced the Shulamite to become a religious person – *keeper of the vineyards*, an obedient and submissive woman: dutifully following protocol. Her rebellion will necessarily lead her to be repudiated by her own; then and there she will obtain, precisely **on behalf of God**, the power to be the keeper of her life.

This is why going from Vashti to Esther is a **regression**; it is going from a faith that is emerging to the law that imposes itself in the name of fear of living. From Vashti's freedom, the text suddenly falls into Esther's religious obedience; which will later on generate, in real life, all sorts of violence and the establishing of political and religious authorities. But the leitmotif and trigger for this fall into Esther is the **law of the couple**: « every man should bear rule in his own house » (1^{22}), the Book of Esther explains. Indeed Vashti the queen, by confronting the king – as the Shulamite had dared confront religious tradition – was breaking a holy and untouchable relogous law. With the coming of Esther, it is a return to normalcy. Women are objects who are getting ready to meet their husband as one meets a god. Esther had been getting ready during no less than a whole year (2^{12}), putting perfume on and taking care of her body for the king's pleasure. In contrast, the Shulamite, awakened in the middle of the night by her lover (God), dares take the plunge into faith (4^{3-8}). Esther and the Shulamite are two opposite worlds; they also represent two different types of couple, as far one from another as are childhood and adulthood. Esther is marriage and the Shulamite is free trust, for « marriage is a religion: it promises salvation but it needs grace », said JACQUES CHARDONNE. Vashti the queen and the Shulamite are precisely about Grace, that is, about a kind of relationship between a man and a woman where trust alone is enough.

By tearing down law and the traditional couple it teaches, we can hear Christ whisper behind the testimony of these two women. The New Testament also bears witness to this, as seen in the contradicting stands of Martha and Mary who are figures for Esther and the Shulamite; and even more with Mary of Bethany whose defence Christ will take against the apostles, directly confronting them; or with Mary Magdalene, the first person to see Christ resurrected. Those Shulamites who were following Christ must have probably endured many upheavals and harsh struggles. Certainly, to have the boldness for a woman to assert her right to sit beside Him so that she may receive from Him as much as a man of faith can receive — that does not go without suffering! And yet what according to you was the greastest suffering these women had to endure? The very same precisely that men of faith endure. Namely, the difficulty – not to say the **impossibility** – to find among Christians a man or a woman who has such a freedom with Christ.

The Church is full of Esthers; housekeepers subjected to the sacred law of those bourgeois couples which become half-hearted over the years. For twenty centuries Christian women have followed Esther, fasting and giving themselves to the bed of their husbands, giving themselves body and soul so that their men would rise to a power the privileges of which they would reap in return. But where are the Shulamites, where are the Vashtis? Must we declare in disillusion together with CHEKHOV: « Give me a wife who, like the moon, will not appear every day in my sky »! Is there still in the world today a Mary Magdalene who is able to **hear** from the Christ what the established Christianity with all their sham apostles are unable to conceive?

The umbilical cord
To Christians

BIRTH IS AN UNPARALLELED EXPERIENCE, all emphatically declare, as it is the very moment when life achieves autonomy at last. For the first time, an infant's mouth will open, air will fill up his lungs, and his navel will close up when the midwife cuts the umbilical cord. However, and we are well aware of it, this experience is not unique in one's life, quite the contrary. Natural birth is indeed like a prophetic scene telling the child, « From now on life will shape you through that same gesture », meaning, to the rhythm of **CONSTANT CUTTINGS** of the umbilical cord. To exist means « to be in the process of becoming », doesn't it? It does very certainly. And the process of becoming does not imply returning into the mother's womb but leaving it so as to become completely free from it!

The newborn baby will have to fight all his life in order to be born into his independence and assert the particular individual he is called to become. Time and again he will have to tear himself away from his biological parents, to gain his autonomy, away from all nests, and to break every fetter. And at each one of his « births » he will feel the air of his newly gained freedom fill up, expand and burn his lungs as he suddenly utters a victory cry. Life here below is a long birth. The biological birth that sets this process going is like a whip lash carrying all the symbols of this life race. It teaches us, moreover, that **EVERY BIRTH PRESUPPOSES A DEATH**, and that « the mother's womb is actually a tomb » because the baby who is being born is also simultaneously dying to the embryo he was.

This constant process of becoming in which life pushes us, this obsession it has of making us an independent being, a Man – that also is a death process life skillfully handles. Life puts to death and condemns, it destroys our dens in which our fears lock us up as change and novelty scare us. Life tears our cords apart then proudly leaves a mark for its gesture in the form of a beautiful scar. In short, life knows from the start that our nourishing cords will eventually wind around us and then – **CHOKE US**!

The same goes for the **SPIRITUAL BIRTH** evoked in the New Testament, which is a constant uprooting of the being. Here also, it is all about cutting the umbilical cords that tie men to various addictions and determinisms. However, while the usual existential process of becoming is about untying an individual from his various ties (his begetters, culture, nation, this or that doctrine or inherited lifestyle, etc.), the spiritual birth that Christ means is in fact an altogether different one. Breaking the umbilical cord in this case means **A SEPARATION FROM NATURE ITSELF** — a complete separation! Therefore, the metaphor of the « mother's womb being a tomb » now refers to **MOTHER NATURE**! In the New Testament, cutting the umbilical cord refers only in a lesser and indirect way to what we commonly call « flesh and blood », by which we mean family, religion, society, or some ideology and its dogmas, ethics and moral codes, etc. Christ means to reach to the very source. He wants to liberate us from our very Nature, from the human being as we know it and which we **PERSONALLY AND INDIVIDUALLY** are. Such a future is out of any common sense and rationality, be it scientific or religious. It is sheer madness. For, in the same way the infant's cord is snipped and then he dies to his embryo existence, this birth process is about tearing man away, not only from his present life, but furthermore from the death towards which that same present life leads him!

The matter at hand is **RESURRECTION**, that is to say a birth out of man, an exit of the *homo-sapiens*. We are here considering a future, a « becoming » that is infinitely more than one of those transformations human evolution is able to trigger. That future is **EXCESSIVE** to man. It is a road that has got nothing to do anymore with the traditional existential progress into which any human wisdom can lead men. It is, from now on, about having man being newly born, awaken to an identity which is impossible to conceive reasonably, an identity the evocation of which is a nightmare to reason, considering that reason's eternal truths will one day have to bow down before this new man. Christ abundantly talked about this being to come, using for that matter the term **SON OF MAN**. By so doing he shed light on a phrase that was already used in the Old Testament. Furthermore, he pretended to be himself the perfect incarnation of a Son of man! And to add to the scandal, he declared that this identity was simply **THE VERY NATURE OF GOD**, thereby making himself God's equal!

This is a far cry from the way the wise and the religious portray those who stand beside their divinity in the after life. Those ones are usually portrayed as angel-looking creatures whose obedience is perfect, that is to say, they are pure consciences, they no longer have personal desires and consequently know no future — they will never become. Between these **Sons of angels** and the **Son of man**, the *homo sapiens*' verdict will of course be as rational as it will be radical: « It is in the logical course of things to be born a *Son of angel*, says he, but to be born a *Son of man* is contrary to reason ». It does not matter that the *Sons of angels* are beings whose nature is actually **totally inhuman**, what matters is that they are just exactly what the evolutionary and sanctifying process of reason produces whenever a human being surrenders to its mechanisms.

Reason shapes a Creature that is refined from every passion and from any proper liberty, a Creature moulded into perfect obedience so as to be turned into a pure conscience. All this, happening in the midst of a world of peace where everything stands in the absolute and final stability of the divine law that sets it.

Let the reader have a clear understanding of the key matter at hand. Which is, that the *Sons of angels* have no need whatsoever to cut mother Nature's umbilical cord because what they become in the after life is only the normal process of their first and only birth, it is its mathematical process. This is why they do not need to be born spiritually. Nature, who is *their nature*, slowly leads them into the Unity of her perfect Law, into the immutability of the divine and into its immateriality, thus, into **her logic of disembodiment**.

This, here, is *not* being born again, it is rather the successful end of the first birth and of the priorities it pursues. The gods that govern this birth lead everything towards what Reason calls *eternal beatitude*, and what man calls death. In opposition, the *Sons of man* are really being born a SECOND TIME since they are clothed with another body, indeed, since they are resurrected! This is why their lifestyle is to cut the umbilical cord of mother Nature, to get out of her origin and to reach their Father's horizon which is the kingdom of heaven. Whereas the *Sons of angels*' lifestyle is to be in communion with their umbilical cord, to follow its way so as to return to their mother's original womb that they see as heaven or as the nirvana.

Oddly enough, it seems that up to today the various strands of Christianity basically agree with this stance on resurrection, with the idea of the new body it promises and of the break from the first one it implies, here below. The Church generally approves of this fact and pretends to firmly believe in it, at least in a theological manner, on paper. So it may be that I am actually only sharing truisms and ideas that other theologians and thinkers have asserted a thousand times, here and there, in the course of Christian history.

Nevertheless, if Christianity so much loves Resurrection why then, for centuries and in its vast majority, has it been so much attached to this world? Why has it been so much absorbed by current events? Why such a determination on its part to serve, to love and to better mother Nature? And why has Christianity taught men that to drink from Nature's best juices and to avidly suck her breast was a divine reward in response to their virtues? Our «succulent reality» yet is the world's womb out of which God is determined to take man. What is more, the world is this *double fear*, this «Egypt» that Scripture talks about: *fear of living and fear of dying*. In the face of such an existence, God offers enfranchisement and **LIBERATION**. From then on, why teach men – in God's name – that the silver cord of our biological and reasonable life is a man's most precious possession? God's work is precisely about **SETTING US FREE** from that earthly cord that our **FAKE-LIFE** is, and his Spirit wants to teach us not to fear mother Nature's Torah, which runs the universe. As a consequence, any spirituality that, «in the name of the Divine», teaches men to drink from the world's breast as a form of spiritual reward — is where precisely lies the diabolical reality. The delicious and appealing diabolical reality has always promised men milk, honey and fat as a reward for their wisdoms. These here are all the spiritualities of the peace prophets, the ones that Scripture repeatedly identifies as «false prophets».

And yet this is the very spirituality that, **IN PRACTICE**, traditional Christianity preaches to its people. Why? Because like all religions, the Church has always wanted to conquer the World and to rule over it. Hence her insistence, her enthusiasm, her ardour to discuss politics, sociology, ethics, justice, the various institutions, culture, public health, and all sorts of policies. Hence her will to discuss the laws that rule our civilisations and her pretence to better them. Hence her intention to develop a discourse, in our technological times, on Ecology! That matter is so much topical that the Church, as opportunist as ever, understands how much the issue can be instrumental in helping restore her image. This is why, these days, we can see a certain strand of Catholicism discoursing on some « divine ecology ». The naive will declare that « the Creation is a temple of flesh and a living house in which God might come to dwell ». In short, Christianity has always been utterly focused on man's happiness here below, it has always thought to be on a mission to manage things « christianly » here below so as to bring happiness and prosperity to its fellow citizens. From there comes the Church's acrobatic splits, which always put her in extreme difficulty. On the one hand, she wants to uphold a philosophy that teaches men the « divine techniques » needed to extract the world's best fruits from its breasts, on the other hand she can see God precisely **ENGAGED IN THE VERY OPPOSITE WORK**! On the one hand, the Church strengthens the cord of rationality through which the « earthy people » are the head of the world and not the tail, and on the other hand she sees God severing that cord and teach His own to **ABANDON RATIONALITY**, to have no fear of offending the motherly soil and of losing its temporal blessings.

However, from the midst of her unhappy imbalance, the Church is perfectly aware of her situation. How then will she be able to hide it? How is she going, for one thing, to go on preaching the new birth, seeing that her existence is founded on this spiritual fact, and for another thing, how will she be able **TO NEVER CUT THE CHILD'S CORD**! Indeed, she fears the moment when a child reaches maturity and becomes passionate about the resurrection more than he is about the Church. In which case he might cut loose and put the ecclesiastic structure in danger. The Church's answer to this dilemma, we must admit, was splendid and craftily devised: « Let us make sure, said she, that we infantilise the individual, but this time on the breast of another mother than mother Nature, who anyway must be put aside theologically. Let us then carve the dogma of **MOTHER CHURCH**. Then, as pagans do with mother Nature, let us say that the Church is sacred and possesses a divine body. Then, every new birth will be consecrated to us and no one will ever dare cut loose from our breast! »

In consequence, Christianity may from this point preach the new birth in a secure manner since its midwives are expressly trained to never cut the umbilical cord. In an altogether different fashion, the cord will even serve as a spiritual diadem. Some will use it as a proof of their spiritual birth, others to boast the special intimacy they have with the divine. As for the oldest, they will see in the cord a sign of their great spirituality and a trophy for their near-sacrificial bond with the Saintly Mother Church, a bond, they think, every Christian is called to possess! We are here in the presence of Christians who have been faithful believers for twenty, thirty or even forty years, but who are still entangled in their umbilical cords. And though they try to deceive their own by turning the disability into a spiritual crown, those Christians are actually spiritual autistic persons, social cases of a sort. They are psychiatric invalids **UNABLE TO TAKE ON THE INDEPENDENCE CHRIST CAME TO OFFER THEM**. If we could see them just for a day through the transparency of pure conscience, they would surprisingly look like children of all ages, and for the less affected, like teenagers.

Still, no one ignores the fact that, one day, the scalpel will work on the skins of us all and the last cord binding us to the living will then be cut for good. On that day Mother Nature will forsake her children to death, and the same will go for all mothers — Science, Nation, Philosophy, Morality, Mysticism, the Church, etc. Or simply for the mother who birthed and raised us. That one, though a human being, is invested with the same powerlessness than the others, and the most heart-wrenching cries of her child being swallowed by death will be to no avail. No mother is strong enough to resurrect her loved ones. Why? Because resurrection is precisely that wedding ceremony the Scripture talks about. It features two persons only, God and the individual, that is, the particular Being each of us is. It is that being, it is **HIM ALONE (OR HER)** who will enter resurrection, just as the bride enters the « Bedroom[1] » **ON HER OWN**. This is how Scripture reveals it in the parable of the shepherd: « Christ calls his own one by one, each by his name, and He takes them out. » (cp. JN 10[3]).

He who has received this bonding relationship from God is then happy for he is on his way towards his resurrection. Is he not saved by this particular intimacy he has with God? And what about those who deny such a freedom to Christians? What about that Church for which a person and another are linked together **MORE** than every-One is linked with his or her God? That Church who thinks God does not lead his own « one by one and each by his name », but that He is leading a herd through a system of harness and yoke

---

[1] In reference to the Talmud which uses the expression « Bedroom » to evoke the « holy of holies », referring to the O.T. Temple.

forcing all animals to march along the same furrow. That ecclesiastic body who poetically and proudly thinks itself a *mother* will know the same end than all mothers. The Church will not save her own because she is wrongly persuading herself for centuries that she is « God's womb », because **SHE PROMISES** to give birth to men's spiritual life. Moreover, she herself will not be saved, meaning, **HER CONCEPT** will have no existence in the resurrection. In the world to-come, the Church professional members will put their hand upon their mouth and be confounded, because the Ekklesia will confirm once more that « in your mothers' love, life makes you a promise at the dawn of life that it will never keep.[2] »

---

[2] ROMAIN GARY, *Promise at Dawn*.

II - SONS OF LAW
(*"them that are perfect"*)

On the Anglo-American religion
To winners

« YOU CANNOT JUDGE MEN by the things they do when they take off their pants. For their really filthy tricks, they get dressed. » Those are the words of Minna, a waitress and a prostitute in *The Roots of Heaven* by ROMAIN GARY. The same opposition goes for Catholicism and Protestantism. The first revelled in his blatant « filthy tricks » to the point that his activities are brought out in the open today with the paedophile scandals. As for the latter, he cleverly knew how to learn his lesson from his brother, so he pulled up his pants and gave himself up to wrongdoings far more outrageous in the end.

Famous sociologist MAX WEBER, on that matter, explains in precise detail the Protestant mindset in his work *The Protestant Ethic and the Spirit of Capitalism*[1]:

> [...] it is a fact that the Protestants [...] both as ruling classes and as ruled, both as majority and as minority, have shown a special tendency to develop economic rationalism which cannot be observed to the same extent among Catholics either in the one situation

---

[1] All MAX WEBER quotes are drawn from the Talcott Parsons translation of *The Protestant Ethic and the Spirit of Capitalism* (1930). Page numbers in brackets refer to the Routledge Taylor & Francis e-library 2005 edition.

or in the other. Thus the principal explanation of this difference must be sought **in the permanent intrinsic character of their religious beliefs**, and not only in their temporary external historico-political situations. (7)

The Reformation, WEBER explains,

> meant not the elimination of the Church's control over everyday life, but rather the substitution of **a new form of control** for the previous one. It meant the repudiation of a control which was very lax, at that time scarcely perceptible in practice, and hardly more than formal, in favour of a regulation of the whole of conduct which, penetrating to all departments of private and public life, was infinitely burdensome and earnestly enforced. (4)

The rule of the Catholic Church, he remarks

> «punishing the heretic, but indulgent to the sinner» as it was in the past even more than today, is now tolerated by peoples of thoroughly modern economic character, and was borne by the richest and economically most advanced peoples on earth at about the turn of the fifteenth century. The rule of Calvinism, on the other hand, as it was enforced in the sixteenth century in Geneva and in Scotland, at the turn of the sixteenth and seventeenth centuries in large parts of the Netherlands, in the seventeenth in New England, and for a time in England itself, would be for us the most absolutely unbearable form of ecclesiastical control of the individual which could possibly exist. That was exactly what large numbers of the old commercial aristocracy of those times, in Geneva as well as in Holland and England, felt about it. And what

the reformers complained of in those areas of high economic development was not too much supervision of life on the part of the Church, **but too little**. (4-5)

The sociologist's analysis is harsh and yet very accurate for anybody having practical experience of Catholicism and Protestantism. But WEBER goes even deeper in discernment. That new religious practice served, according to him, as a lever for the establishment and the domination of the capitalist spirit in Europe. Quoting a peer, he says that «**the Calvinistic diaspora was like the seedbed of capitalistic economy**» (10).

Among numerous examples in his detailed work, he takes that of BENJAMIN FRANKLIN, a founding father of the United States. Born in Boston, FRANKLIN was the son of an English immigrant and was bred in the Puritan tradition. «His strict Calvinistic father drummed into him again and again in his youth: "Seest thou a man diligent in his business? He shall stand before kings." (Prov. xxii. 29)». (19) FRANKLIN, who later became at a denominational level a «colourless deist», according to WEBER, left an autobiography from which the scholar extracted the following lines in order to support his study on the Protestant ethics:

> **Remember, that time is money. […] Remember, that credit is money**. If a man lets his money lie in my hands after it is due, he gives me interest, or so much as I can make of it during that time. This amounts to a considerable sum where a man has good and large credit, and makes good use of it. **Remember, that money is of the prolific, generating nature**. Money can beget money, and its offspring can beget more, and so on. Remember this saying, The good

> paymaster is lord of another man's purse. He that is known to pay punctually and exactly to the time he promises, may at any time, and on any occasion, raise all the money his friends can spare. This is sometimes of great use. After industry and frugality, nothing contributes more to the raising of a young man in the world than punctuality and justice in all his dealings; therefore never keep borrowed money an hour beyond the time you promised, lest a disappointment shut up your friend's purse for ever. (14-15)

« Truly what is here preached is not simply a means of making one's way in the world, but **a peculiar ethic** », Max Weber comments. He adds, « the infraction of its rules is treated not as foolishness but as **forgetfulness of duty**. » (17) Then he goes on describing a telling aspect of this mentality:

> Now, all Franklin's moral attitudes are coloured with **utilitarianism**. Honesty is useful, because it assures credit; so are punctuality, industry, frugality, and that is the reason they are virtues. A logical deduction from this would be that where, for instance, the appearance of honesty serves the same purpose, that would suffice, and an unnecessary surplus of this virtue would evidently appear to Franklin's eyes an unproductive waste. And as a matter of fact, the story in his autobiography of his « conversion » to those virtues, or the discussion of the value of a strict maintenance of **the appearance of modesty**, the assiduous belittlement of one's own deserts in order to gain general recognition later, confirms this impression. According to Franklin, those virtues, like all others, are only in so far virtues as they are actually

useful to the individual, and the surrogate of mere appearance always sufficient when it accomplishes the end view. It is a conclusion which is inevitable for strict utilitarianism. (17-18)

But WEBER does not stop with this criticism which, alone, would leave FRANKLIN in the typical attitude of the hypocrite. « But in fact the matter is not by any means so simple. BENJAMIN FRANKLIN's own character, as it appears in the really unusual candidness of his autobiography, belies that suspicion. The circumstance that he ascribes his recognition of the utility of virtue to a divine revelation which was intended to lead him in the path of righteousness, shows that something more than mere garnishing for purely egocentric motives is involved. » (18) For, he adds, concerning the Protestant mindset at large: « A lack of care in the handling of money means to him that one so to speak murders capital embryos, and hence it is **an ethical defect.** » (144)

« And in truth, » the German sociologist insists,

> this peculiar idea [...] of one's duty in a calling [...] It is an obligation which the individual is supposed to feel and does feel towards the content of his « professional » activity, [...] is what is most characteristic of the « social ethic » of capitalistic culture, and is in a sense the fundamental basis of it. [...] The ability of mental concentration, as well as **the absolutely essential feeling of obligation to one's job**, [...] This provides the most favorable foundation for the conception of labor as an end in itself, as a [spiritual] **calling** which is necessary to capitalism. (26)

We could conclude these series of quotes, lengthy but essential to get an idea of MAX WEBER's discourse, with this last word by the economist:

> [...] the characteristic Protestant conception of the proof of one's own salvation, the *certitudo salutis* in a calling, provided the psychological sanctions which this religious belief put behind the *industria*. But that Catholicism could not supply, because its means to salvation were different. (152)

✿

For almost five centuries, this Religion has been completely permeating the Anglo-American, Dutch, Swiss and, for a large part, German mentality and spirit. All these peoples are insidiously led by that asceticism in work, by that financial prosperity brandished like a divine seal, like the evidence that some exceptional moral justice will reward the individual person: it works as a stamp which validates a so-called «divine election». That spirit is to be found absolutely everywhere in the activities of the Protestant populations. As for «artists» or for those who boast about being on the margins of religion, all those who, in the midst of Protestant societies, flatter themselves to be in direct opposition with their religious background, those who declare loud and clear to have freed themselves from it, the truth is they just cannot get rid of it. Indeed, this manner of hero worship, worship of the virtuous man or of the romantic conqueror, actually has its source in the Protestant religious background they pretend, yet, to have overcome. The Protestant ethic has weaved its precepts in the shadow of their souls and it is still brought out in their lifestyles and their social reflexes without their realising it. The fervent atheism promoter just like the « rebellious » music artist, the avant-garde writer or the « wonderful » world of movies, etc.: all actually partake in it. Every TV series, every novel is filled with the smell, more or less strong, of that Protestant thought which introduced these peoples into the modern age before any other. **These societies are circumcised to the ethic of financial success as a reward** and the American system so much overindulged in it that it reached to an ultimate frenzy when it engraved the motto « In God we trust » on its banknotes!

But the realm in which this painless poison reaches its shiniest modernity, the moment when it stands out in majesty, is when it seizes the Bible! There, to quote Minna, men and women « pull up their pants and adjust their skirts », dress modestly, put perfume on and wear their best polite smile, then they go and commit the « filthiest tricks »: **the evangelical teaching!** Today love of money, the capitalist spirit, and security in the name of God are brought to new heights. Some sophisticated trick, that strikes the right balance, that is all dialectics and rhetorics, has Christ say he is a friend of Mammon. If Peter is the apostle of Catholicism, Paul that of Reformation Protestantism, then Judas is the apostle of modern Protestantism. This is only normal, for Judas was **an accountant**. One still wonders why countries such as France, with so many thinkers of value and so much ability for critical thinking, are constantly at the feet of these gold and glitz lovers. From now on, the churches of Europe seem to share in that same love, that same gold, that same fever for happiness and comfort that **the Bible yet almost always denies its anointed**. European Protestantism also – as it went on listening to those false prophets, as it went on being bitten by their « Gospels » in which the rewards of the god-Good are made of money, of well-being whereas, they declare, the punishments of Evil bring poverty and insecurity – that Protestantism is now but the legitimate son of some pagan Christianity. The time and the circumstances are getting near. The day is coming when Christ will hand them the bread he handed Judas in order to reveal his deepest intentions. I doubt that before that day French Protestantism will wake up and kick the asses of all these Anglo-Saxon missionaries and authors. It will probably share, with all these Mammon-god saints of the useful and successful, in the same tree where Judas hanged his greed. The Protestant's shame will come after the Catholic's. The younger brother who thought he was more cunning than the elder eventually defeated the theatre of the antique episcopalian masses: he knew how to make the ropes invisible by conforming more intimately to the world.

A quick word on Billy Graham
To the Evangelicals

THERE IS SOME FORM OF PROTESTANTISM, in Europe and on other continents, utterly addicted to and spellbound by the American evangelical preaching. This is a seriously worrying attitude. It is strangely reminiscent of the propaganda used to describe WWII historical facts. Indeed, we are taught from childhood that America, like a saviour, has rid Europe of Nazism. We know however that just like France, Italy or Great-Britain, the total American casualties came to about half a million men. Next to those, Russia lost more than **20 MILLIONS** of her people, thousands of kilometers away from the much-hyped Normandy landing that History focusses on. Whereas millions of Slavic men and women were being sacrificed in a kind of incognito, not to say of contempt on the part of the average European for whom victory could only be celebrated on an American tune, Russian people were nevertheless taking down HITLER on their own, thus paving the way for his permanent defeat in Europe.

But propaganda worked splendidly. Awestruck Europe turned to the west and praised America the hero. Since then Europe has been opening up to the American way of life, her mouth wide open in bliss, feeding on all America's messages and welcoming her messengers on the red carpet. Nowadays the same blindness is working on the mindset of some form of Christianity, like a shadow. Christians turn to the west as if over there exclusively Christianity possessed the secrets of evangelical victory. As if God had endowed the *made in US* ecclesias with a spiritual power capable of defeating humankind's enemies. Christianity from across the Atlantic is considered a model of excellence, naively and almost with idolatry. Is it not the first one to reach the ultimate goal of that messianism we pretend to be perfectly faithful to Christ? Meaning Christendom must **REIGN** politically!

In his documentary *With God on our Side*, DAVID VAN TAYLOR tells us about the RICHARD NIXON election. The freshly elected President is standing before the excited audience and the usual clique of journalists. By his side on the podium, a smile topped with falcon's eyes, is standing BILLY GRAHAM. The religious preacher is given the microphone and immediately delivers in Old Testament tones, « O God, we consecrate RICHARD MILHOUS NIXON to the Presidency of these United States [...] We pray this humbly in the name of the Prince of Peace who shed His blood on the Cross that men might have eternal life. Amen. » At that moment NIXON was experiencing an ecstasy unlike any other. Just imagine! he was no less than being directly enthroned by God Himself through the mouth of one his most prestigious evangelists. At that moment in time, both were convinced to be on a divine mission — they would lead the most powerful Nation in the world to once again **save** it from a devouring invader.

The old Roman Pope of Old Europe was then being floored, together with his *urbi et orbi*, his « to the city and to the world ». As for Pope of Protestantism BILLY GRAHAM, there he was, raising the *urbi et orbi* up to the level of divine hopes. It is true that the anointing has changed hands. Nevertheless, BILLY GRAHAM was the worthy son of the Bishop of Rome for, much the same as him, GRAHAM's aim was to reign politically and he spoke with bombast *to the city and to the world*. However the American preacher, a much more pragmatic man, easily outdid his father. Leaving the old liturgical outfit, he dressed in a suit cut by the best tailors, studied modern economy and the workings of Mammon, to eventually make his way into the very exclusive circle of political dark powers. He then shook hands on a regular basis with *exousia*, with « powers » — there, at the top step of their glories. What about Christ? He did the exact opposite as he disowned all authorities and publicly mocked them (cf. COL 2^{15}). Christ threw their crowns to the ground, shouting to the world and to the city, « My kingdom is not of this world [...], now is my kingdom not from hence » (cf. JN 18^{36}). Without doubt, **CHRIST WAS NOT ON THE PLATFORM WITH BILLY GRAHAM** and RICHARD NIXON, he was absent from such a place. One day, the American preacher will need to account for the way he took possession of the name of the son of God in order to build his human fantasies and, on top of this, for having led into them so many gullible crowds that listened to him.

In the face of such a corruption of the Gospel, the word of CHESTERTON springs to my mind, « The modern world is full of the old Christian virtues gone mad ». The political domination of Christianity is merely the tragic and pathetic mix of Judaism and the Gospel. It is Peter stammering in awe at the transfiguration and talking nonsense, « Let us make three tabernacles; one for you, and one for Moses, and one for Elias » (Mc 9⁵). It is that old fearful move of an immature Christianity that wants to sew Faith and Law together. That is to say to make God a tangible reality, to blend the Christ with a theocracy coming from the Law, to force him, as did the pharisees and the crowd, to accept a political enthronement. Happily enough, the Nazarene preferred the cross and the incognito of resurrection. **CHRIST DOES NOT WANT TO RULE OVER MEN!** He wants to change their nature so deeply, so thoroughly that every-One rule over their own reality, that they be king or queen of their own kingdom — that they be neither with God nor Master. Christ offers himself as Father, and he is himself the Father who is self-sacrificing for his sons, but never is his final goal to give himself as an Almighty God to sons who could only get near him on their knees. He has in view their full freedom. He wants to take them from the position of creatures subjected to their Creator to that of the dignity of sons wearing their Father's nature. This is a radically different thing. It is an authentic break from the Torah theology with its social morality. It is a divorce without return from that fervour the Old Testament has to be politically interpreted and to rule over men.

🖋

But has not BILLY GRAHAM preached the Gospel? some might ask. Has he not led numerous persons to Christ? Let us not be so positive. It is an easy thing to generate intellectual or moral conversions, which are typical of political conversions after all. You use the power of suggestion on someone to form convictions in his mind with the captivating lever of a talented speaker and his campaign manager, an expert in propaganda. You want to learn manipulate these or those values and mechanisms that work on the human psyche, so that you acquire on that someone enough power to make him take the ballot paper you want to see him use. This is how the «specialist in conversion» can exert such an authority on his neighbour and make him believe he chose it freely. In fact, there is no election on neither sides. Here only lies a moral and intellectual manipulation which is **IN NO POSSIBLE WAY SPIRITUAL**!

As a matter of fact, it is easy to see a conversion of the conscience to a given pattern of Good *&* Evil thought and **CONFUSE** it with spiritual birth, which is precisely outside all good *&* evil patterns. Indeed, the Spirit works altogether differently. It literally comes and tears down the person, it drives him mad. It precisely makes it impossible for the moral or intellectual quibble to stand any longer so that it no longer offers a way out for that person, who cannot have but one hope: the hope of a completely free, miraculous and unreasonable intervention of God. All this occurring in an intimate and personal one-on-one meeting between man and heaven. The Spirit's intervention is beyond good and beyond evil. Beyond any reason, any logics, any theology and any justice. The Spirit has to do with the Justice of the Kingdom of heavens which no eye has seen, no intelligence has grasped, no feeling has experienced. This *counter-Torah* justice which makes a man be born of God cannot be comprehended in any human way. We need an all-gracious action on the part of Christ so that suddenly would open for man this *brand-new* he had never imagined before, this *brand-new* he now can only embrace and make his through Faith alone.

But what do preachers with their BILLY GRAHAM principles do? They equip themselves with some human charisma that they crown with some wise men morality, then they shape the humanist personality within the excellence of a well-suited theological training. Finally they wrap it in a carefully elaborated esthetic universe. In the end, the whole thing is neatly inserted in a show for the crowds where the media effect surrounding people works to convince them they are living an extraordinary moment. Proud of their work, these preachers thus suppose they can reach the same goals than those of the Spirit even though the Spirit **IS ABSENT**! The imitation of the Spirit is so well done that it is enough to exalt an audience member. Alas, an audience member is often very easily exalted. He believes in it. And from there on he embarks in a conversion that he thinks is a spiritual one, when it is only intellectual or sensual, and unfortunately largely human.

Such is the religious process, such its power, such its seduction. Catholicism's archaic liturgy and the old Protestant rigorism have cleverly transformed into evangelical Masses. Since then, people say that these modern religious theatres from the west are carrying off the spiritual victory of the Gospel. But nothing could be further from the truth. The real victory is taking place behind that story, in real History. It is taking place in another land and thousands of *spiritual* kilometers away from that media hype of the divine. Victory is gained by those inspired individuals whose faith weighs one thousand times more in heaven's eyes, but who are nonetheless being sacrificed under the media pressure of the « triumphant » ecclesia, far from podiums, platforms and applause. In that precise place where the Spirit dwells, far from gatherings and street audiences. In the simplicity of a meeting with one's neighbour, in the intimacy that a man or a woman may have with God in the secret of their room. In the **INCOGNITO**, as KIERKEGAARD liked to say. « As soon as a crowd forms, God becomes invisible. And this all-powerful crowd may go and hammer at his door, it will not go any further, because God only exists for the individual. That is His sovereignty. »

In his book *Hope in Time of Abandonment*[1], JACQUES ELLUL talks about **ABANDONMENT**. Abandonment is God's silence, it is His absence.

> It is my belief, ELLUL explains, that we have entered upon the age of abandonment, that God has turned away from us and is leaving us to our fate. Of course I am convinced that he has not turned away from all, or rather, I think that he may be present in the life of an individual person. He still may be the one who speaks in man's heart. But it is from our history, our societies, our cultures, our sciences, our politics that God is absent. He is keeping quiet and has shut himself up in his silence and his night. (71).

Then he further adds about religion,

> It is collectively that we experience God's silence and his absence: it is the body of Christians, the churches, people in the aggregate who find themselves aban-

---

[1] JACQUES ELLUL quotes are drawn from the C. Edward Hopkin translation of *Hope in Time of Abandonment* (1973). Page numbers in brackets refer to the Wipf and Stock Publishers 2012 edition.

doned. And the personal experience of a few ones does not change anything about it. (125).

In the third part of the second chapter entitled « Signs of Abandonment in the Church », ELLUL writes more precisely about what he calls « dryness ». *Dryness,* for him, is « the lack of outreach in witnessing, the lack of transmission of the Christian message » (139). The evangelisation principles of BILLY GRAHAM and the like take root in that dryness. Little by little, JACQUES ELLUL comes to the specific example of the American evangelist.

This *dryness,* he explains, is a combination of the religious spirit and « the great effort on the part of Christian intellectuals to make the message audible, comprehensible and acceptable on a purely natural level » (140). JACQUES ELLUL then condemns *the exegesis of progressive annihilation and of dissection of the texts.* « The more we dissect a text, the less will it be accessible to a fundamental understanding. The more one improves his formal knowledge of the text, the more its basic significance vanishes. » (142-143) He goes on explaining,

> It is true that, with God absent, the only thing left for us to do in our real spiritual poverty, is to keep peeling the layers from the textual envelope. We can rest assured, however, that that will lead nowhere. Its only effect will be to confirm our sterility and to make it more obvious. It is not a matter of jumping to the opposite conclusion and saying: « Let us not perform any more exegesis. Let us regress to a naïve and fundamentalist reading » [...] it becomes harmful when we pretend to get out of the impasse by means of exegesis, and to do without the Holy Spirit while

going after the same result. The hermeneutic enterprise probes tirelessly and ever more deeply into the mystery of the possible communication and recovery of meaning (142;144)

He then further analyses the workings of the hermeneutic enterprise:

> It makes one's head spin. It is the exact equivalent, in reverse, of ancient metaphysics. Strictly, it is a matter of putting oneself in the place of God's decision. It is a matter of making Scripture alive and meaningful without God's making it alive and meaningful. It is a matter of effecting the transition from Scripture to word, or of making language into the word, by putting together highly sophisticated human means in order to economize on the use of the Holy Spirit. Hermeneutics is the business of interpreting revelation without revelation. [...] Consequently, God is forbidden to speak. God does not need to speak in this matter, it's up to ourselves to make him speak. We need to substitute our hermeneutics of the word for his word. (144)

As he eventually refers to our specific case, ELLUL declares the following, « BILLY GRAHAM's propaganda methods are the exact equivalent, at his level, of the hermeneutic philosophy in that they use every last means to obtain results which the Holy Spirit is no longer giving. One can obtain conversions by propaganda thereby economizing on the action of God, just as hermeneutics can obtain a meaning. » [without it being God's meaning]. (146)

The first edition of *Hope in Time of Abandonment* dates back from 1972! Jacques Ellul, the man from Bordeaux, published nearly 60 works the content of which reflects the best wine in the world that is to be found in his home place. However, Christendom will prefer to quench their thirst with sweet drinks served by preachers from across the Atlantic. Let no one wonder today. The Church has sacrificed an inspired man who was standing at her gates. She carries within herself intellectual, emotional and moral converts, the result of those sham preachers motivated by Billy Graham style propagandas. That is to say the Church is overflowing with men and women whose spiritual birth, if it ever happened, now reveals individuals suffering with every sort of spiritual psychiatric ailments. **Must we cry over her?** For the time being, let her drink from divine abandonment, from God's silence and from his absence. In that place, Ellul said, « there is a huge thrust towards faith, for it is that misery of a man crying out to an empty heaven which can call God to life. » (191)

On hymns
To the happy

In his work *The language of the Third Reich*, Victor Klemperer explained how Nazi propaganda would daily modify German language so as to spread its ideology. He notably said that totalitarian mental oppression was made of « mosquito bites, not big blows on the head ». It is a mixture, he went on, of « Novalis and Barnum ». Novalis referring to the Romantic poet and Barnum to the American show business entrepreneur who created the Barnum circus in 1871.

Psychologist Paul Meehl coined the phrase « Barnum effect » from there. He was alluding to the manipulative skills of the circus man who declared that « a good circus must have something for everyone ». The *Barnum effect* designates a suggestion, a subjectivity. Through those, a person is led to accept the fact that a brief description or a fleeting impression apply exactly to his personality. The *Barnum effect* is to indulge in wishful thinking. It is the disturbing trend of giving a meaning to all our experiences. From there, bitter hopes arise. These suggestions work on the intelligent and the stupid alike. Astrology, cartomancy, numerology and other kinds of spiritualities make an excessive use of it. Via theses practices, customers are convinced that they are assessing their life and their personality in some sort of meeting with «truths» that are uttered and felt. They enter some belief which is suggested to them as being unquestionable and certified. Any challenging of their practices or experiences would be from then on deemed «blasphemous».

That mixture of suggestion (barnum) and romanticism (novalis) is typical of churches. And it has been so for centuries. Paganism, with its spiritual shows, produced the very first movie screenings. It also used to manipulate its inevitable «**CLIMAXES**». That moment, thus called by movie professionals, occurs when cinematographic tension and emotion reach a paroxysm. This is when the action resolves in a response also called *crux of the plot*. ARISTOTLE was talking of **CATHARSIS**, (from *katharein*, meaning «to purify, to purge»). The term was first used during religious expulsion rituals practiced in Antiquity. For SOCRATES, PLATO or the STOICS, catharsis and philosophy are linked. It meant to isolate the soul from the body, to kill the particular being and dissolve it into the general idea. Closer to home, however, apart from the term used in psychology, catharsis refers to **THE SPECTATOR'S FUNDAMENTAL PLEASURE**. During climax, a sort of emotional purge is taking place, a therapeutic release. It is the scenario's conflict resolution: David kills Goliath. Screen writers and communication professionals are perfectly familiar with the mechanisms of catharsis. The spectator is made to think that he is that hero triumphing in his fight against evil.

THIS IS HOW ANY RELIGIOUS PERFORMANCE WORKS. Catholicism started with its Latin recitations in spectacular buildings, among its own actors wearing special clothes for the occasion. The created suggestion, with its liturgical romanticism, combined with the purification of the participant's conscience — all of this yielded huge takings the world over. But Catholicism is moribund. Protestantism skillfully managed to modernise the show, to transform it so as it would stick closer to our reality.

And this is why music and hymns, more than prophecies, sentimentalism or miracles, are such crucial elements today. A successful church is one that sings the best and that uses best the modern technologies of sound and light. Just like the Old Testament, which is full of hymns and liturgies, notably in the glorious age of the Kings, churches are coming forward to conquer souls. Trumpets in hands, they suggest to their people that they are the breed of the saints come to make the world a happier place and to make its feelings blossom.

COUNTER TO THIS RACKET, the New Testament is as stingy with hymns as the Old is generous. Apart from three paltry references in the Pauline letters (among which Ephesians and Colossians, precisely suspected to be pseudepigrapha), we have nothing! Revelation, which is about the world to come, needs to be considered separately of course. By contrast, in the one and only occurrence where the Gospels refer to hymns in Christ's presence, what is then being said is utterly meaningful. Indeed, after the text reads, « And when they had sung an hymn, they went out into the mount of Olives », Jesus himself speaks and announces: « All ye shall be offended because of me this night » (MAT 26$^{30\text{-}31}$).

Bang! The inevitable happened. The disciples fell asleep during prayer while Christ was sweating blood. Then they all left him! Finally Peter denied him and the cock crowed. All this occurred in the hours following the singing of hymns. The real New Testament Hymn is the cockcrow! That is the message of the text. Great author GOGOL was writing about the cock, *whose shrill crow always heralds weather change*[1]. Is the New Testament not heralding the changing of time? Is it not announcing that man's nature will be revealed? That man, singing at the top of his dunghill, needs to learn who he is so he can reach what he is not.

Looking at Masses and all the evangelical «circuses», such a man has come to wonder what could God be possibly thinking about it. Now, can he not see what VICTOR KLEMPERER could see? That is, « **THE MOSQUITO BITES** » of religious propaganda through which it is suggested to one, in a sickly romantic environment, that their sanctification is the purgative experiment of worship services and Masses. There is more truth in Peter's bitter tears than in the hymns he was chanting the moment before. Let Christians do the same, let them cry bitterly. For, today, their hymns and their prophetic jumble are tolling their reprobation. They are themselves the prophecy that they cannot hear for screaming so loud. **THE PROPHECY OF THE COCKCROW THAT IS SOON COMING FOR THEM.**

---

[1] NIKOLAÏ GOGOL, *Dead souls*, Book II.

A geometry of Eden
Based on Genesis 2-3

ON READING THE FIRST CHAPTERS of the Bible, we can easily see what makes philosophers smile over the *garden of Eden*. Truly, these people have always held on to the principle PLATO displayed on the pediment of his Academy, « Let no one ignoring geometry enter. » And the description the Bible gives us of the garden of Eden includes a geometry mistake even our soberest logic would not silence.

Even so, the biblical text is at first rather accurate. It tells us how God began to choose a place on earth, the Eden, then marked out inside that place a space called *the garden*. There He placed a man. Moreover, we are told, a river having its source outside came flowing into the vast enclosure of the garden where it divided itself into four arms, their names are even given us together with geological and geographical data about them. And while the author is describing the three tree species growing in this habitat, he takes the opportunity to indicate its centre, **THE CENTRE OF THE GARDEN OF EDEN**:

> And out of the ground made the LORD God to grow every tree that is pleasant to the sight, and good for food; the tree of life also **in the midst** of the garden, and the tree of the knowledge of good and evil. (GEN 2[9])

Readers mindful of coherence will therefore be reassured with the description of this *apparently* well-organised space. Nothing seems to be missing for a peaceful and enriching life, and its centre, like a king-axis, is clearly defined by the famous «Tree of life». The presence of a vital centre is an utterly cheering detail as it suggests no one will be given over to some mess that could be distressing. Hence, we are allowed to think that, at this stage of the reading, PLATO's maths and *ratio* buff disciples need not be suspicious of this biblical metaphor for **THE ORIGINAL NAKED SOUL**, which is what the «garden of Eden» is. It is the place where «Adamity», that is mankind, took its roots. Consequently, this is a way for the biblical text to evoke the place where it all began for the individual being!

And yet, as the author goes on, he leads us into a geometrical aberration which insidiously appears in his narrative. For, we surprisingly find ourselves with a «second centre»:

> But of the fruit of the tree [of knowledge] which is **in the midst** of the garden, God has said, You shall not eat of it, neither shall you touch it, lest you die. (GEN 3³)

While it seems God had indicated the centre of the garden to be where **THE TREE OF LIFE** is located, his calculation is bluntly checked by Adamity.

Adamity is just beginning to become aware of itself, to discern its differences and its potential. And when its intuitive, so-called feminine part converses with its luminous and learned part represented by the serpent, mankind will suddenly focus the centre of Eden in the place where the **TREE OF KNOWLEDGE** is planted. And there we are, like fools, with two centres on our hands: **AN IMPOSSIBLE THING**!

Indeed, there is a geometrical conflict. But how could philosophers use this conflict to accuse the biblical text of being frivolous and consequently reject its testimony? As geometry lovers, should they not, on the contrary, take this narrative very seriously? Precisely because Adam and Eve have achieved a « clever coup d'état » and because the couple was bold enough to establish Knowledge **IN THE CENTRE**, these wisemen should see that they are dealing here with the same sort of mankind they belong to – they are reading about the very **FIRST** Academy students!

For not only did the couple reject the initial idea which exhorted them to keep the Tree of Life in the middle, but they furthermore rejected the divine **BAN** on feeding on Knowledge in order to manage life. These zealous defenders of the Tree of Theories are definitely the forefathers of all scientists, ideologues and dogmatic people of all time! They too, this Adamic couple, considered the primacy of Life too abstract and subtle a thing to leave it to the judgement of the naive. Adam and Eve thought, like our thinkers and intellectuals, that it would be a disgrace if Life was to rule on its own at the centre of everything, left to its own devices and offering itself for free consumption with no other restriction than personal and arbitrary liberties. How could such a highly precious good – Life – be **FREE** and so uneconomical?

How could one abandon such a treasure to the sole hazards of private cravings with no security access that would be impersonated by a learned, modest and strict universal keeper? And so this is how they policed Life! They subjected its free access, and our freedom, to a strong-arm, rational and brilliant principle: **Knowledge**, with its order of merits and rewards. From then on, every man would enjoy from life what is strictly due to them, and according to obvious, clear-cut and collective standards, no room left for randomness. Only what is insignificant would be left to its own personal and subjective strength. Men would be controlled, threatened and then finally educated with subtle shrewdness. Little by little, each of us would have to *freely* accept that no morsel of our liberty escape from the rulings of luminous and scholarly Reason *within ourselves*. And whenever Reason commands us to justify ourselves, we would have to present proof which are geometrically admissible.

This is how the ideologies of Good and Evil have come to judge the Tree of Life. **That Tree is no longer in the centre**, it has been moved to the fringes. More importantly, it has been entrusted to sublime keepers who dispense its benefits – no more freely and according to the own free judgement and appraisal of the *existing-man* – but according to his merits, according to some table of laws, that is, according to his work and his submission. The compass and the scales now measure obedience and ethics, and the most disciplined ones are awarded prosperity and a title of authority. As for the very essence of Life, that is, the Spirit, for which living means to be incarnate – well, its madness has left life. It has gone. Life then lost its majesty, and existence was given over to chaos. What a bargain for Reason! For she hastened to subdue Nature's vitalism, that chaotic power. And this is how existence became *a coming and going of life and death*, an endless struggle that never allows Reason to enter in the rest of her Sabbaths.

And last, the concept of **ETERNITY** has been abundantly explained by wisemen from time immemorial. It is that metaphysical frame of *Eternal Truths* they relentlessly strive to discover and engrave on their tables of scientific and religious laws.

Thus, *actual-Life* split up with life; it split up with man. It left him. This is why the *tree of life* we are fed here below, by Nature and by the Gods of Theories, is but a placebo of that other-Life. It is an allegory, a pipe dream, a false hope, a biological vapour evaporating day after day from our being. Death defeated life because our logic defeated our madness.

PLATO's Academy motto – *let no one ignorant of geometry enter* – was then devised by men as life's golden rule from the beginning: **IN THE BEGINNING WAS FEAR OF GEOMETRY!** And the biblical text seems to tell us that this is precisely what prompted God to drive Adamity out of the garden! The Grecian creed is therefore displayed on the way out's pediment, and it is at the same time the slogan of our entrance into our present life, here below, in this altered Eden which our mortal incarnation is — that reprieved *corporeal Soul* into which we have entered when we could have been a Spirit: *we could have been Life.*

We incarnate ourselves in a vast Academy where all are gripped by the fear of being bad geometers for, in this place, we find out that a single step can take us from delight to torture. This is why everyone tries to cultivate the Tree of Certainties to extract **GOOD** out of it, blind to the fact that good and evil come out of the **SAME ROOT** and feed on the same sap. And wisemen, like any good geometer, know very well that for any given space there can only be one and one centre only: **THE UNIVERSAL**. For this reason, the divine will makes them smile. Because the Tree of Life will never reign. It will never be in the centre.

Wisemen argue rightly that individual life is too animal to be left to freedom – to Life. They bewitch the whole world, convincing everyone that doctrines and ideologies have the power to transfigure beasts, *our individualities*, and to turn them into **ANGELS-OF-THE-UNIVERSAL**. In so doing they save man but by killing him. They abolish man who is absorbed in the angel! Century after century, as every human shoot comes to be grafted on the Tree-of-eternal-truths, it is the whole of earthly Eden which finally tends to be absorbed by this captivating and « knowledgeaholic » centre. And thus that centre leads the world to its perfection; to the meeting point where all places and the middle will be One; where no more space of liberty will ever be; where every small shoot of life will have for blood scientific data made of algebraic and electromagnetic values: the blood of death. Indeed it is death oozing from the tree of knowledge. It is the tree of death. Its truths scrupulously and conscientiously suck up freedom, the arbitrary, the sudden, the improbable and the impossible. These truths dry up green wood with their seductions, then they even do the same to dry wood. They everlastingly burn an « eternal self » by enclosing it in its indisputable evidences so as to turn it into a fossil insect trapped in its amber.

May God have mercy on us! May he sow in our hearts the seed of his Tree of Life. May he grow in the secret garden of our soul the vine stock of his Life. Then shall we have the courage to lay the axe to the root of the Tree of death where our lives are measured and weighed in preparation for our burial. What is more, we know exactly where to go to delight in his tree of Life. Over there, where he erected it: at the Golgotha. Over there where the cup of the warm blood of the One who is resurrected flows. Then and there man will be **THE MEASURE OF ALL THINGS**, whether SOCRATES likes it or not, meaning he will be king of his garden which itself will be resurrected into a divine kingdom – where **THERE IS NO PLACE FOR WHOEVER IS NOT KING.**

You don't believe it? In that case allow me to tell you one last thing. Namely, that the *Geometry of Eden* was from the beginning absolutely accurate. It is in truth God himself who gave man the Freedom to choose his own « life centre ». Therefore there are not *several centres*, but *several possibilities of truths* that may work as command centre: this tree or that other tree. Indeed we can very well translate verse 9 of chapter 2 quoted above this way:

> And out of the ground made the LORD God to grow
> [...] the tree of life also in the midst of the garden,
> **with** the tree of the knowledge of good and evil.

A number of translations agree with this when they use « with » instead of « and » (Versions in French: LEMAISTRE DE SACY in 1701 or ZADOC KAHN in 1899, for example). Let me then repeat. From the moment we are reading the text in this manner, the author no longer places us before a bad geometry issue with two impossible centres. No. He pretends God is growing two Trees on the same spot! It is even more harebrained!

For, you see, if you decide to cultivate, here below in your edenic invisible, the Tree of Life, it will begin to make the Tree of Knowledge which rules in this world **EXPLODE**. This way, you will create for yourself a reality over there where «everything will be possible to you», because your **LIFE AS A SON OF GOD** will be the centre, because **YOU WILL BE THE TRUTH AND THE LIFE**, and because the Tree of Knowledge will be uprooted from your Eden and placed in an outside environnement as a mere servant. If however you cultivate, here below in your edenic invisible, the Tree of Knowledge, you will probably manage to get a good harvest on earth since Reason rules in our world. But — you will nip the Tree of Life in the bud! Hope therefore that there is no life after death for then you shall be received in the icy shade of the dead Tree. And seeing the Tree at last in all its bareness, without the masks of reality, **YOU WILL KNOW EVERYTHING, BUT YOU WILL BE NOTHING**, having no more life. Is this not miscalculation?

EPILOGUE

From disciple to ambassador
Based on Luke 14 $^{25\text{-}33}$

Luke 14 $^{25\text{-}33}$

^{25} And there went great multitudes with him: and he turned, and said unto them, ^{26} If any man come to me, and hate not his father, and mother, and wife, and children, and brethren, and sisters, yea, and his own life also, he cannot be my disciple (one of those who learn with me). ^{27} And whosoever doth not bear his cross, and come after me, cannot be my disciple. ^{28} For which of you, intending to build a tower, sitteth not down first, and **counteth the cost**, whether he have sufficient to finish it? ^{29} Lest haply, after he hath laid the foundation, and is not able to finish it, all that behold it begin to mock him. ^{30} Saying, This man began to build, and was not able to finish. ^{31} Or what king, going to make war against another king, sitteth not down first, and **consulteth whether he be able** with ten thousand to meet him that cometh against him with twenty thousand? ^{32} Or else, while the other is yet a great way off, he sendeth **an ambassage**, and desireth conditions of peace. ^{33} So likewise, whosoever he be of you that forsaketh not all that he hath, he cannot be my disciple.

« You must be able to give up all your belongings if you want to learn with me », Christ dared assert. *Excessive demand! Outrageous! A speech that pervades every fundamentalism!* Is it not the first thought that crosses our minds on hearing such a speech? Unless we dare not admit it. Anyway, the Church perfectly smelled the danger since these words by Christ are in direct conflict with the « ideology of the family » that any religious minister fights tooth and nail for. This is why the Church has cleverly reversed the trend by asserting the exact opposite: « Christ is an obliging master who wants to wrap up your life in goodness and love; he has plans of happiness for you. This is why he tells you, *If any man come to me he will reign down here, his prosperity will expand, he will be the head and not the tail, and men will look upon his success as a model.* What you only need to do is give up your sins and then be faithful to the Church and its morals. » This way, we think we are putting Christ back on track and improving the Gospel by removing its fundamentalist fragrance. However that **earthly rule** the Church promises is certainly a prospect that not only exudes and trickles of religious fundamentalism, but is particularly vain.

Fundamentalism is what makes the difference between the words of the Church and those of Christ. Fundamentalism being on the Church side. Does Christ make the promise to lose everything? Clearly not. He promises resurrection. And indeed, it seems to me that the least of things needed to resurrect is to die, whereas the fact of « losing everything » is precisely what is particular to death and to its ideology. To learn about resurrection is in fact to learn giving up everything, it is also learning to die! Who would be such a fool so as to promise resurrection without **THE CONDITION** of dying, that is, deny we must concretely be deprived of everything beforehand, and only then, take back a hundredfold?

And yet the Church promises just this, and this is where her religious fundamentalism lies. « The promise of resurrection begins here below in a concrete manner, says she. For, being a Christian means experiencing the increase of wealth and earthly success as **SIGNS** of the heavenly vocation. And with facts so self-evident, God inevitably leads unbelievers to convert and join the ranks of the ekklesia. » It is on that mere basis that, for centuries, the Church has been selling herself to winners and their policies. She thus approves of their countless wrongs and their ethnic cleansings, arguing that the World must enter in the Christian sheepfold by the arm of the strongest. Is it not a spiritual fact that she is standing on the side of the mighty, the happy and the rich since, according to her, victory is the sign of resurrection?

In the end, what distinguishes these two ways of reading Christ is that one understands him according to Law and the other according to Faith. Law is a fulfilled promise, or rather a process the fulfilment of which must be manifested visibly and in reality. Whereas Faith is a promise the fulfilment of which is as certain as it has **NO EVIDENCE**. Its only evidence is an empty tomb as, indeed, what Faith promises is absolutely not of this World. « My disciples own the world », says Law; « Therefore they have their reward, answers Faith, but my own will infinitely possess some wealth that your own will see go to waste into death. »

When a disciple of Law becomes aware of that promise of infinity, he naturally wants to embrace it, therefore he will start building it in the present reality, that is, according to methods that are specific to Law. With the cement of the letter. He then sets out to follow Christ, often **EN MASSE**, while preciously keeping Law and its magic formulas in his backroom. Then suddenly appears a powerful army sent to destroy his construction. Taken aback, he does not understand that the tower he has built does not belong to faith. He cannot realise that faith's construction is always invisible and hidden. Moreover, he cannot see that it is **HIS LUST FOR RESURRECTION** which has just brought that destroying army upon him. To follow a promise that is not of this world, it is of course to leave the promises of this world along the way and to abandon them to the forces of death, but mostly, it is to have faith that all these *defeats* are but an illusion. The peculiarity of resurrection is to take back everything and to recreate everything in a boundless nature.

Consequently and at that moment, the disciple of Law is sad and scared. He is presented a choice that gives him away! What will he do? He will hurriedly go and consult Law to know how to get out of this trouble, how to protect his tower, that is, how not to lose what constitutes for him the visible sign of the coming resurrection. « Send an ambassage to these kings », the laws of reason cleverly suggest him, « you will offer them a large part of the riches of faith and then you will rule **TOGETHER** over the promise of heaven. You will be like God here below! United to powers like these ones, you will henceforth be able to convert all the kingdoms, obtain all the riches and carry out here below, in the midst of humankind, that messianism of happiness you have been entrusted with. » Thus a religion is born. Thus was born the Church. She was born in the apparent humility of a fearful ambassage. She is being born at the moment when, for man, the prospect of losing all that is paramount to him here below does not arouse enough faith in resurrection to embark on such a risk. The ambassage, it is the Church and it is, Christ was saying, « desiring conditions of peace with death » (verse 32).

Let the reader not be troubled by such a tragedy. Let him not be troubled when people mock him because he stops building with religion, because he renounces what makes his heart's delight, and that which are his most precious plans. What matters is to build with Christ a tower in the invisible – **THAT PART SHALL NOT BE TAKEN AWAY FROM HIM**. One day all prestigious towers must collapse, all delights from here below, and all ecclesiastic glories. One day the Church must hear the angels' gibes. As for these hidden towers of faith, these divine temples buried in every-One, they will appear one day for what they are. They will be a surprise even to those who carry them, as they will see and hear, « This is what your Father was pleased to give you, because the kingdom of heaven, it is you, it is in you. The endless possibilities are from now on in you. »